Penguin Education

Penguin Modern Psychology
General Editor: B. M. Foss

Developmental Psychology
Editor: B. M. Foss

Males and Females
Corinne Hunt

Corinne Hunt
Males and Females

Penguin Education

Penguin Education
A Division of Penguin Books Ltd,
Harmondsworth, Middlesex, England
Penguin Books Inc, 7110 Ambassador Road,
Baltimore, Md 21207, USA
Penguin Books Australia Ltd,
Ringwood, Victoria, Australia

First published 1972
Reprinted 1973
Copyright © Corinne Hutt, 1972

Made and printed in Great Britain by
C. Nicholls & Company Ltd
Set in Monotype Times

For John

Contents

Editorial Foreword

This is a scholarly work on a topic which is often treated in a sensational or biased manner. It is a topic in which it is difficult to disentangle biological and cultural influences. People have expectations regarding the roles which men and women should play, and individuals live up to these expectations to varying extents. In doing this, their very physique may be affected, an effect which looks as if it should have had a biological cause. Corinne Hutt is sophisticated about these interactions between biological and social factors, and steers the reader with caution and objectivity.

The plan of the book reflects this biological–social polarity. It starts with genetic and physiological factors and finishes with a consideration of men and women in society. The first three chapters provide an excellent primer for anyone wanting to be initiated in an authoritative way into the origins of sexual dimorphism and other kinds of differentiation. Dr Hutt then discusses sex differences in sexual and non-sexual behaviour. Her own highly original work on child behaviour has obviously sharpened her perceptive and critical approach to this as to other sections. There is a short, up-to-date account of 'intersex' conditions, and chapters on the differences in abilities of the two sexes, and in their social motives. The book ends with a section on the equality and inequality of the sexes in which Dr Hutt stays very close to the evidence. The chapter has the virtues of a source book, but is lucid, and at times provocative through its unwillingness to take sides.

It should be expected that someone with a rigorous training in animal ethology should be able to take a steadfastly scientific approach to the biological aspects of the subject.

Dr Hutt is also a wife, mother and professional woman and is obviously deeply concerned with the place of women in society. Above all, as the reader will quickly discover, she is determined to get the facts straight.

B.M.F.

Preface

My interest in sex differences is of relatively recent origin. It was aroused by some quite unexpected findings obtained in studies of the exploratory behaviour of pre-school children. These results showed that, even by three or four years of age, many boys and girls engage in characteristically different patterns of exploration. Attempts to understand these results and to interpret them plausibly inevitably led to a consideration of the genetics and neuroendocrinology of sexual differentiation. I appreciate the generosity of Christopher Ounsted and David Taylor in permitting me access to their contributions to the edited volume on Gender Differences prior to its publication (1972).

In the preparation of this text I was helped by many people and I wish to acknowledge their contributions: Jill Watson prepared the illustrations of our protocols with great sensitivity; the arduous task of preparing the manuscript and figures and compiling the index was skilfully undertaken by Betty Green; the detailed comments and helpful suggestions of Geraldine Frank, Frances d'Souza and my husband John, improved the text immeasurably.

Silas meditated a little while in some perplexity. 'I'll tie her to the leg o' the loom,' he said at last – 'tie her with a good long strip o' something.'

'Well, mayhap that'll do, as it's a little gell, for they're easier persuaded to sit i' one place nor the lads. I know what the lads are; for I've had four – four I've had, God knows – and if you was to take and tie 'em up, they'd make a fighting and a crying as if you was ringing the pigs. But I'll bring you my little chair, and some bits o' red rag and things for her to play wi'; an' she'll sit and chatter to 'em as if they was alive. Eh, if it wasn't a sin to the lads to wish 'em made different, bless 'em, I should ha' been glad for one of 'em to be a little gell; and to think as I could ha' taught her to scour, and mend, and the knitting, and everything. But I can teach 'em this little un, Master Marner, when she gets old enough.'

George Eliot: *Silas Marner*, 1861

Above all, she lived in contact with a masculine mind, listened to how a man talked, studied his tastes and motives, the unworthy as well as the good; watched his passions and his responses to pleasure, noted how different they were to her own or her sisters', and recognized how seldom he acted from disinterested motives or from simple kindness, and even less from motives of duty. Now he was a grown man, there was hardly any particular in which Branwell resembled his sisters; while his pretensions were far greater than theirs, his resolution to attain his desires was immeasurably weaker. Such as he was, Emily would not judge him.

Winifred Gérin: *Emily Brontë*, 1971

Introduction

In recent years there has been a resurgence of interest in the topic of sex differences, although it is a topic that has been well documented in the psychological literature for nearly half a century. The recent interest in the differences between males and females is no doubt due to the efforts of certain movements directed at social change. An unfortunate consequence of this source of renewed interest seems to be the tendency to refer to such differences, only to dismiss them as cultural excrescences, or to demonstrate the creation of male and female stereotypes by society.

Having met, repeatedly, with rejections of any suggestion, however covert, that some human sex differences may be of biological origin, it seemed important to set the 'sexual differentiation' story in perspective. This is what I have tried to do in the present volume. In much developmental and social psychological writing too little cognizance is taken of the structure and function of the brain, much less of the constraints set by the nature of its organization. I make no apology, therefore, for stating the case for the biological bases of psychological sex differences.

The first two chapters deal with the chromosomal and hormonal determinants of sexual characteristics. Males and females differ in every cell – every mammalian male cell has a sex-chromosomal complement of XY and the female of XX. The effects of the male and female sex hormones determine that physiologically the sexes function very differently. In considering the process of sexual differentiation as it occurs in early development (chapter 3) it is clear that the basic mammalian template is female. It is male differentiation which is actively organized by the androgenic hormones; female differentiation occurs by default, as it were.

The next chapter discusses sex-typical patterns of behaviour, both sexual and non-sexual and the attempts to elucidate the mechanisms of their control. The evidence strongly suggests that at the outset males and females are 'wired-up' differently. Social factors thus operate on already well-differentiated organisms – predisposed towards masculinity or feminity. The cases of abnormal sexual development discussed in chapter 5 afford further support for this differentiation. The development of normal boys and girls, from infancy throughout childhood to puberty, is characteristically different (chapter 6); this fact has several implications, some of which are educational.

Chapter 7 reviews the human sex-differences that are manifest in intellectual skills and other aptitudes, and chapter 8 discusses differences in attitudes, interests, values and emotions. In the final chapter I have tried to consider the implications of these differences for male and female roles in society. Since, in many respects, these are complementary to each other, their description in terms of 'superiority' or 'inferiority' can only be with pejorative intent. A society that exploits such differences is likely to benefit more than one that is procrustean towards the sexes.

In the course of this volume I have referred frequently and extensively to animal experiments, but I am aware of the difficulties of direct extrapolation to humans. In general, however, the readiness with which we accept or reject the results of animal experiments depends on how well these accord with our preconceptions. Were it not for such results, our knowledge and understanding of the structure and function of the brain, the actions of drugs, the mechanism of genetic coding, the processes of learning and attachment, would be primitive indeed.

1 The Genetic Determination of Sex

The sex-chromosomal composition of men and women

Every cell of a human being, from conception to death, contains forty-six chromosomes, twenty-three of these being contributed by each parent of the individual. The chromosomes align themselves in pairs, a paternal chromosomes pairing off with the homologous maternal chromosome. Twenty-two of these pairs carry genes that determine certain bodily and other features of the individual and are called *autosomes*. The members of an autosomal pair are very alike in size and structure. These twenty-two autosomal pairs are usually arranged in order of decreasing size to form a *karyotype* or graded sequence, consisting of seven groups for purposes of identification. The twenty-third pair of chromosomes are the sex chromosomes and consist of XX in the case of a woman and X Y in the case of a man.

The X-chromosome is quite large, about seventh in descending order of size. The Y-chromosome, on the other hand, is very small – often smaller than the smallest autosome. Moreover, whereas the X-chromosome is known to carry several genes, only one structural gene has so far been associated with the Y-chromosome – one resulting in hairy ears. Genes borne on the sex chromosomes are referred to as sex-linked genes. A mother can only endow her offspring with an X-chromosome. Thus it is the father who determines his offspring's sex: if a sperm bearing an X-chromosome fertilizes the ovum the result is a girl, if a Y, the result is a boy. Since a father can only transmit a Y-chromosome to his son, sex-linked characteristics can never be transmitted from father to son. Thus a haemophiliac father cannot produce a haemophiliac son, but could, through a 'carrier' daughter, produce an affected grandson.

There are several consequences of the differences in the sex-chromosomal composition of men and women. One of these is the greater susceptibility of the male to a number of recessive disorders. In the human species, most characteristics are the cumulative effects of several genes. For example, even eye-colour or hair-colour is under the control of two or three genes. Only some diseases are known to be controlled by single genes. Such genes very often are also recessive genes, being manifest only in the homozygous condition, i.e. when *both* chromosomes – the one inherited from the mother as well as that inherited from the father – carry the recessive gene. In the case of recessive genes carried on the X-chromosome therefore, e.g. haemophilia or colour-blindness, a female will only manifest the condition if both her X-chromosomes bear the gene. More frequently, in the heterozygous condition, she will be a carrier, since the effect of the recessive gene will be masked by its dominant counterpart on the other X-chromosome. The male, on the other hand, having only one X-chromosome, will manifest the disease even in the monozygous condition, since the Y-chromosome contains no genes which are the counterparts of those on the X-chromosome. Hence there will be far more male sufferers of such sex-linked disorders than female, even though the transmitters of such diseases will always be the females. It is thought that there are about seventy X-linked traits in man, many of them pathological and recessive. In the case of X-linked dominant genes of course, both males and females are affected.

Sex-linkage must be distinguished from sex-limitation. In the latter case, the genes are not carried on the sex chromosomes but are only manifest in one or other sex. A good example is that of baldness, which is a sex-influenced gene only manifesting itself in males, since for its operation it requires the hormonal conditions characteristic of a male. Thus it may manifest itself in a heterozygous woman who develops a masculinizing tumour of the ovary.

One consequence of the discrepancy in size of the X and Y chromosomes is that the female technically has more genic material than the male. Since the X-chromosome in man is supposed to contain almost 5 per cent of the DNA of the nucleus (Federman, 1967), the excess of genic material in the female is considerable. Generally, when there are quantitative changes in the amount of chromosomal material – an excess as in the trisomy conditions or a deficit as in the monosomy conditions – such changes are associated with characteristic deformities, both physical and mental. One of the commonest of these chromosomal abnormalities is that associated with one type of mongolism (Down's syndrome) – trisomy-21, i.e. three instead of two chromosomes 21. In the case of excess chromosomal material, the greater the excess the more severe the disorder. Thus trisomy-13 is considerably worse than trisomy-21, chromosome 13 being larger than chromosome 21 (Lejeune, 1967). This principle, which applies to the autosomal material, does not appear to operate in the same manner with the sex chromosomes. The fact that the mammalian female has more genic material than the male has no adverse effects in itself; nor does the double 'dose' of an X-linked recessive disorder in a homozygous female result in a more severe disorder in the female than in an affected male with only one 'dose'.

The hypothesis put forward by Mary Lyon of Harwell (1962) helps to account for the somewhat unusual behaviour of the sex chromosomes. It had already been discovered (Barr and Bertram, 1949) that, at a certain phase in cell-division, a darkly staining body could be observed in the nuclei of female cells. This sex-chromatin body is referred to as the Barr-body. Males do not have a Barr-body in their cells. Investigations of the sex-chromatin in cases of sex-chromosomal abnormalities show that the number of Barr-bodies appearing in a cell is one less than the number of X-chromosomes in the genotype. Thus, in a normal male with the sex-chromosome composition XY, or in a case of Turner's syndrome XO, no Barr-bodies are seen, but an XXX individual will have two Barr-bodies in her cells. Lyon suggested that in normal circumstances only one X-chromosome is active in any cell, the other X-chromosome(s) becoming genetically inactive, compressed and staining as the Barr-body. This process begins early in the development of the embryo, and in any single female cell, Lyon suggested, it is a matter of chance which X-chromosome is inactivated – the one inherited from the mother or the one inherited from the father. Once one of the X-chromosomes has been inactivated in a cell, all the products of the division of the cell would have the same X-chromosome inactive. This hypothesis thus allows for compensation for the disparity in size and contents of the sex chromosomes between males and females: due to the inactivation of one of the X-chromosomes, the female has no more *active* genic material than the male, and since, on average, only half of the total X-chromosomal composition is active in a female, a homozygous recessive condition for example, is no worse than the equivalent heterozygous condition in the male.

The Y-chromosome and male development

The genetic determination of sex, strictly speaking, goes only as far as the formation of the male or female gonads – the testes or the ovaries (the rest of the process of sexual differentiation is under hormonal control). In mammals, it is the Y-chromosome that organizes sexual differentiation according to a particular pattern. In the presence of a Y-chromosome cell division in the zygote appears to be speeded up and the medulla or inner portion of the embryonic gonad (sex organ) proceeds to differentiate into a testis (Mittwoch, 1971). This happens during the seventh week after conception. If differentiation of the testes fails to occur in the seventh week, then the cortex or outer part of the primitive gonad differentiates into an ovary. The Y-chromosome, therefore, plays an important part in initiating and actively organizing the formation of the male gonads. If it is present, masculine development will take place despite the presence of several X-chromosomes as in the sex constitution of XXY, referred to as Klinefelter's syndrome, or even XXXXY. The presence of the Y-chromosome cannot be masked by X-chromosomes, however numerous. On the other hand, in the *absence* of a Y-chromosome, feminine development takes place. The X-chromosome does not apparently play any active role in directing sexual development in a particular manner. It seems that nature has provided that when the equipment necessary for masculine differentiation is lacking, development shall proceed according to a feminine pattern. We shall see that this is so even where hormonal influences are concerned.

Genes do not control behaviour. They control enzymes, which affect biochemical processes, which in turn may affect structures and functions at various levels of complexity. The Y-chromosome, for instance, not only determines masculinity but confers a 'male' flavour upon human development. One of the ingredients of this characteristic flavour is a vulner-ability to all manner of traumata. On average 120 males are conceived for every 100 females. At term the ratio is 110 males to 100 females and in terms of live births the ratio has de-creased to 106 to 100. This means that the majority of spon-taneous abortions or miscarriages, many of which are due to chromosomal abnormalities, are of male foetuses. Male infants are also more susceptible to perinatal complications such as lack of oxygen. Throughout life the human male remains more vulnerable to a variety of disorders such as cerebral palsy, febrile convulsions, viral infections, ulcers, coronary thrombosis and some forms of mental illness. In fact his longevity is so curtailed that by the sixth and seventh decades of life the sex ratio is reversed in favour of the females. The adage of the male being the stronger sex seems to be limited very much to physical strength! Potts (1970) has recently provided a good review of this topic.

The greater vulnerability of the male has been hitherto one of the less explicable features of development. In an attempt to account for this fact, as well as other related phenomena such as the slower maturation of the male (chapter 6) and the greater variability in a number of male features and functions, Ounsted and Taylor (1972) have put forward an hypothesis concerning the function of the Y-chromosome. Their theory, briefly, is as follows: the Y-chromosome carries no genetic information itself but nevertheless elicits more genetic in-formation from the genome since the range of phenotypic expression of a particular trait is greater in males than in females; the increased genetic 'read-out' is made possible by the slower development of the male. The authors provide a helpful analogy:

... the task of development is like a child mounting a spiral staircase. As males climb the staircase they tread on every stair and find on each step some instructions which they must follow. The process of development takes them repeatedly over similar territory, each replication at a slightly higher level than before. Each instruction, basic to their development, takes time to fulfil. Females enter a directly comparable staircase, the equivalent information is potentially available but the instructions include advice to proceed at a faster pace. To achieve this she will miss out certain steps and ignore their information. Compared at any standard time after setting out the male and female will be in different loci with different amounts of information. Whether one or the other is *better* or *worse*, more or less *advanced* or *retarded*, is irrelevant, but will depend upon what is being measured. What is certain is that it will be different.

A good example of the operation of the Y-chromosome in this manner is shown in Table 1: with respect to stature, the presence of the Y-chromosome enables more of the genetic information to be expressed, an extra Y enhancing this process further. The Turner's syndrome female (XO) is of extremely short stature; although the presence of an extra X-chromosome does not substantially increase the stature of the female, the presence of one or more Y-chromosomes results in a significant increase.

Table 1 Height and numerical anomalies of sex chromosomes (from Polani, 1970)

Type	Number	Mean height in cm
45, X	128	141·80
46, XX		162·20
47, XXX	30	163·07
46, XY		174·70
47, XXY	118	175·69
48, XXYY	22	180·52
47, XYY	19	182·95

If more genetic information is expressed in a male, it follows that more disadvantageous as well as more beneficial traits will be manifest – hence, in the distribution of I Q scores for example, males predominate at the extremes (see chapter 7). Furthermore, due to the slower maturation of the male, the period of risk for a number of adverse experiences, both physiological and psychological, is extended, and hence the number of male casualties is increased.

Although the mechanisms whereby the Y-chromosome regulates development and genetic expression arc still un-known, this theory is both parsimonious and biologically satisfactory.

Chromosomal anomalies

The sex chromosomes are implicated in behavioural distur-bances too. Surveying a number of studies Polani (1970) found that in special hospitals with maximum security nearly 5 per cent of the inmates were males with chromosomal anomalies. These chromosomal conditions were found in only 0·25 per cent of the general population. The largest subgroup of these chromosomal anomalies consisted of X Y Y 'supermales'. These men have an extra Y-chromosome and are often very tall, very impulsive individuals, usually becoming delinquent at a very early age. Such men constitute a fractional proportion (0·06 per cent) of the general population but form nearly 3 per cent of the inmates of maximum security hospitals. The 'super-male' description of the X Y Y individual has recently been questioned by Money (1971) on the grounds that many such individuals have homosexual associations by choice. Money describes these men as impulsive and explosive rather than aggressive and as unable to defer gratification to the future.

An extra X-chromosome – in X X X females – has been found to occur with an unexpectedly high incidence in a hospitalized schizophrenic population, whereas the absence of an X-chromosome (X O) seems to be associated with juvenile delinquency (Kaplan, 1967). No such X-chromosomal ano-malies were found in a volunteer control group. The associa-tion of sex-chromosomal abnormalities with behaviour deviations of one kind or another does not of course mean that the presence or absence of a chromosome *causes* such a disturbance. But just as the organism is often not able to tolerate physically the addition or deletion of autosomal material and is thus non-viable, so also with the addition or deletion of sex-chromosomal material, the organism, though more tolerant of it, is nevertheless more at risk.

2 Hormones in Male and Female

Two systems regulate, coordinate and integrate the multitude of functions in animal organisms – they are the nervous system and the endocrine system. The nervous system functions by transmitting impulses from receptors, via the brain or spinal cord, to effector organs. The endocrine system, on the other hand, consists of internal glands or organs which secrete their characteristic chemical substances, hormones, directly into the blood stream. Because the hormonal messages are transmitted via the vascular system, every tissue, indeed every cell of the body, with the possible exception of the cortex of the brain, is eventually influenced by these. Endocrinology is the study of these 'ductless glands' and, more importantly, their secretions, and the effects of these hormones on metabolic processes.

Traditionally, the study of endocrine function and that of nervous system function have proceeded independently of each other. More recently however, the interdependence of the two systems has been acknowledged in the far more interesting and challenging area of neuroendocrinology.

Endocrinology, in some form or other, has an impressively long history. The Greeks were greatly concerned with the humours and the characteristic temperaments associated with them – the melancholic, the choleric, the phlegmatic and the sanguine. In 350 BC Aristotle described the effects of castration upon the cock, and from prehistoric times to the present century the belief that the consumption of the testicles of virile animals, or occasionally even of one's fellow-men, would increase a man's potency, was exploited commercially with success. An interesting and informative account of the history of endocrinology is given by Greene (1970).

The trusted, and sometimes exceptionally powerful, eunuchs of ancient Egypt and Rome, the castrati singers of the Baroque and Classical periods, the docility of neutered domestic animals, the increased weight of the castrated cock or turkey, all offer evidence of the pervasive action of the male hormones on functions other than purely sexual ones.

The endocrine glands of the human male and female are shown in Figure 1. Of special concern to us here will be the gonads (ovary and testis), the adrenals, and the pituitary,

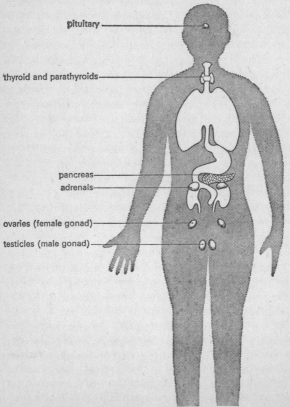

Figure 1 The endocrine glands of the human (from Greene, 1970)

since it is the functioning of these organs that are differentially implicated in the two sexes.

The male gonads and hormones

The male hormones, that is, those hormones having a masculinizing action, are collectively termed *androgens*. The chief of these, testosterone, is secreted by the interstitial cells of the testis which lie in between the tubules in which the spermatozoa are produced. Thus the testis has a dual function: to produce sperm in the tubules, and to produce the male hormone in the interstitial cells. In the human male androgens are secreted even prenatally, and this testicular function can proceed without being accompanied by the production of sperm. The latter function, however, is not independent of the former since androgen appears to be necessary for the maturation of the sperm.

Although the testis produces androgen prenatally, it was thought there was postnatal inhibition of this testicular secretion until puberty. But the breakdown products of the testicular hormones can be detected in the urine of very young children and it is considered that there is only a *relative* decrease in androgen production postnatally, gradually rising throughout later childhood until puberty, when there is increased and constant secretion of the male hormone, as well as the production of sperm.

The female gonads and hormones

The ovary, like the testis, also has a dual function – to produce the ova and to secrete the female hormones. Whereas the testis secretes only one type of male hormone, chiefly testosterone, the ovary secretes two distinctive types of female hormone – the oestrogens and progesterone. Of the several oestrogens produced, the principal one is oestradiol. The oestrogens are produced by cells of the ovary rather similar to the interstitial cells of the testis. The ova develop within follicles which lie in the outer layer or cortex of the ovary. At ovulation the follicle ruptures, releasing the ovum into the fallopian tube and thence into the uterus. The cells of the empty follicle then grow and proliferate and develop into a new and temporary endocrine gland, the corpus luteum. It is the corpus luteum which secretes progesterone.

The oestrogens help in the growth and maturation of the reproductive tract – the oviduct, uterus and vagina. They stimulate growth of the muscle coat of the uterus and the development of the mammary glands. Progesterone, on the other hand, is the gestational hormone, essential for pregnancy. It promotes the further development and thickening of the endometrium of the uterus in preparation for implantation of the ovum, should it be fertilized. Progesterone also stimulates the activity of the secretory cells of the breasts. If the ovum has not been fertilized, after about two weeks of progestogenic activity, the production of progesterone ceases, the endometrium of the uterus is shed and menstruation occurs. This cycle is repeated roughly every twenty-eight days.

These hormones of the sex glands do not function independently, but are under the control of hormones (gonado-

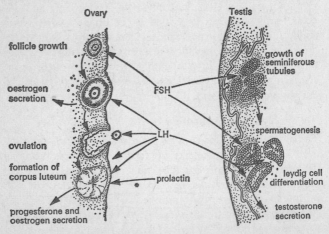

*This effect of prolactin on the ovary occurs in the mouse and rat but not in other species. An effect of prolactin on the gonad of male mammals has not been demonstrated

Figure 2 Actions of pituitary gonadotrophins on the ovary and the testis (from Frye, 1967)

trophins) released at higher levels – the pituitary gland and the hypothalamus of the brain. The actions of the gonadotrophins on the gonads are illustrated in Figure 2.

Higher control of the sex hormones

The hypothalamus is an area of about the size of an acorn at the base of the brain, and is concerned with the regulation of hormonal functions; it is also involved in the regulation of motivational and emotional aspects of behaviour. Below the hypothalamus is the considerably smaller pituitary gland (Figure 3), and it is the anterior part of the pituitary which is of principal concern to us here. The anterior pituitary secretes several hormones: the gonadotrophic hormones (GTH) which regulate the release of the sex hormones and are referred to as the follicle-stimulating hormone (FSH), the luteinizing hormone (LH), and prolactin; the growth hormone (GH); the thyrotrophic (or thyroid-stimulating) hormone (TSH); and the adrenocorticotrophic hormone (ACTH).

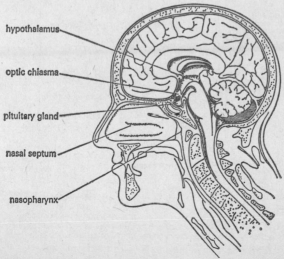

Figure 3 Section through the head to show the position of the pituitary gland (from Greene, 1970)

The sites of action of these anterior pituitary hormones are outlined diagrammatically in Figure 4. FSH is primarily concerned with the production of the ovarian follicles in the woman and of sperm in the man; it also stimulates the ovary to secrete oestrogen. In women, LH causes maturation of the

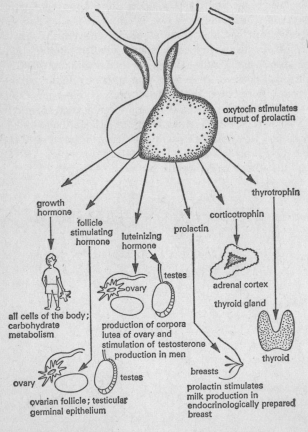

oxytocin stimulates
output of prolactin

thyrotrophin

growth
hormone

follicle
stimulating
hormone

luteinizing
hormone

prolactin

corticotrophin

testes

ovary

adrenal cortex

thyroid gland

all cells of the body;
carbohydrate
metabolism

production of corpora
lutea of ovary and
stimulation of testosterone
production in men

thyroid

ovary

testes

breasts

ovarian follicle; testicular
germinal epithelium

prolactin stimulates
milk production in
endocrinologically prepared
breast

Figure 4 Sites of action of the anterior pituitary hormones
(from Greene, 1970)

follicle and ovulation and subsequent formation of the corpora lutea. Once formed, the corpus luteum functions as an additional endocrine gland and secretes progesterone. L H stimulates the production of testosterone in men. Prolactin stimulates lactation.

Growth hormone helps build up tissue, thereby promoting growth, and T S H controls the activity of the thyroid gland. A C T H stimulates the cortex of the adrenal glands to secrete corticosteroids like cortisol and corticosterone, which are necessary for the individual in withstanding stress and shock.

These hormones of the anterior pituitary gland are themselves released at the command of the hypothalamus, which discharges the respective releasing factors into the blood supply connecting it to its chief executive, the anterior pituitary. The whole system of hormonal secretions maintains a delicate homeostatis. This is achieved by means of negative feedback which operates in the following manner. Suppose that for some reason – perhaps anticipation of a road accident – there is an increased secretion of A C T H from the anterior pituitary regulated by the hypothalamus, and consequently a surge of corticosteroids from the adrenal glands, into the blood stream. The hypothalamus registers this increased level of steroids, and damps down its secretion of corticotrophin-releasing-factor to the anterior pituitary, which in turn inhibits this gland's secretion of A C T H. Reduced A C T H means less stimulation of the adrenals and hence less production of corticosteroids. In this manner the hormonal system adjusts itself to its normal functional level. The same principle applies to all hormonal circuits.

The operation of this negative feedback is of course jeopardized by the removal or non-functioning of any one component in the circuit. For instance, some cases of goitre, or enlarged thyroid, occur endemically where there are iodine deficiencies in the diet. Iodine is taken up by the thyroid and metabolized, and therefore a deficiency impairs the functioning of the thyroid. Since the thyroid is not secreting its hormones, the anterior pituitary releases more T S H in order to stimulate the thyroid. This results in structural enlargement of the thyroid but with no improvement in its function. The vicious circle continues until the deficit is remedied by the external administration of iodine.

From what has been outlined already, it can be seen that the female is hormonally more complex than the male: she produces three gonadotrophins and two quite different gonadal hormones. All the gonadal hormones, as well as those released by the adrenal glands, are steroid hormones – that is, they have a characteristic chemical structure. To complicate matters further, the adrenal glands also secrete androgens and oestrogens, but in small amounts; the testes also secrete small amounts of oestrogens and the ovaries secrete some androgen. However, the androgens secreted by the adrenals and the ovaries are far less potent than the testicular hormone, testosterone itself.

Not only do the ovaries function differently from the testes but the higher neural centres of the hypothalamus which control the secretions of the sex hormones also function differently in the male and the female. Except in seasonally breeding mammals there is a tonic or fairly constant output of gonadotrophins and hence androgens in the male; in the female these outputs are phasic or cyclic. This important difference is inherent in the way the hypothalamus is organized during some critical period in development. This single fact, that *some part of the brain is characteristically different in males and females*, is one of the most significant findings in neuroendocrinology.

Other effects of the sex hormones

Apart from the effect the sex hormones have on the reproductive tract and secondary sex characteristics, they exert an influence on many other non-sexual functions by the action they have on enzymes and metabolic processes.

Testosterone, for instance, is an anabolic steroid, i.e. it promotes the synthesis of proteins from fat and amino acids. It facilitates the retention of nitrogen, potassium, calcium and phosphorus. Thus it promotes tissue growth and repair, particularly in muscle and bone; these effects also occur in the liver, kidney and brain (Greene, 1970). Athletes are known to have taken androgenic substances in the hope of increasing their physical prowess.

Oestrogens and progesterone, on the other hand, appear to have a catabolic effect, i.e. they encourage the breakdown of proteins. The administration of progesterone to male rats results in an increased excretion of amino acids in the urine. Oestrogens make it more likely that dietary fats are metabolized and localized in adipose tissue; they also control the placement of this fat deposition since females become rotund in quite characteristic locations. Oestrogens facilitate weight gain, usually through retention of water. This fact is exploited in the treatment of livestock prior to slaughter: beef cattle receive regular injections of oestrogen for several weeks before slaughter and show remarkable increases of weight, due largely to water retention and alterations of the connective tissue. Most women show fluctuations of weight during the menstrual cycle, the increases occurring at ovulation and just prior to menstruation, when the level of oestrogens is greatest.

Paradoxically, oestrogens cause a decrease in fatty substances in the blood. Up to the age of fifty, white American men have a far higher serum cholesterol level than women (see Figure 5), and are correspondingly more prone to coronary disease and atherosclerosis (Bierman, 1969). The rise in female serum cholesterol levels after the age of about fifty is probably due to the menopausal cessation of oestrogen secretion.

Oestrogens tend also to facilitate glucose metabolism and often have a beneficial effect on diabetic conditions, whereas androgens reduce carbohydrate tolerance and exacerbate diabetes. The role of progesterone in this respect is much more equivocal. The oestrogens can also interfere with liver function, primarily by causing a reduction of bile flow (Kappas and Song, 1969). Although normally the levels of oestrogen are sufficiently small not to affect hepatic function too adversely, in pregnancy, and with certain brands of oral contraceptives, the levels of hormone are high enough to have a considerable effect, thus resulting in jaundice. In fact, many cases of subclinical jaundice – where liver function is impaired, but not to an extent sufficient to produce clinical symptoms – have come to attention after women have taken a contraceptive pill for some months. The jaundice in newborn babies is the result of the mother's difficulties with bile excretion during the latter part of pregnancy.

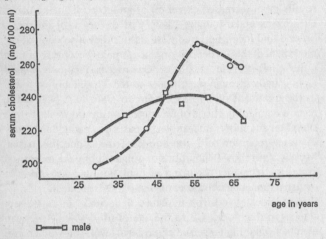

Figure 5 Change with age of serum cholesterol levels in urban white adult males and females (from Schaefer, 1964)

An interesting role of the sex hormones is their differential effect on the metabolism of certain drugs and foreign substances. Particularly after puberty, there often are marked sex differences in the response to drugs – males metabolizing a drug more rapidly than females (Gram and Gillette, 1969). This action is due to an increase in enzyme activity in males at puberty. If barbiturates are administered to males and females, the females will sleep longer than the males. The same effect is seen with rats. Thus if male rats are treated with oestrogen their enzyme activity is reduced, whereas treatment of female rats with testosterone greatly enhances enzyme activity. The metabolism of certain drugs can also be much impaired during late pregnancy or by some forms of contraceptive pill.

From an early age oestrogens slow down growth, probably by some inhibitory action on the production of growth hormone by the anterior pituitary, since animals treated with oestrogen are dwarfed in size (Brown and Barker, 1966). At puberty, when oestrogen is secreted in appreciable quantities, it actively stops growth of the long bones, and consequently prevents any substantial addition to stature.

The sex hormones, we have seen, have many effects other than those on sex organs and functions, and it is often as a result of these non-sexual effects that we may observe a characteristically 'feminine' or 'masculine' response in matters other than those concerned with reproductive function.

At puberty

It is at puberty that the anterior pituitary secretes the gonadotrophins which cause the gonads to secrete the sex hormones. In both male and female characteristic changes in many features take place. As androgen production increases in the male, the genitalia increase in size, and pubic, axillary and facial hair appear. The hair at the temples recedes, giving the characteristic male hairline. Formation of muscle and bone protein is increased, resulting in increases in weight and height. The skin coarsens and sebacious glands increase, often causing acne. The voice deepens and there are increases in both sexual and aggressive drives.

At menarche in the female, the pituitary secretion is chiefly FSH which stimulates the secretion of oestrogen which is responsible for many of the changes at puberty. Linear growth stops, but due to the deposition of fat, the bodily contours become rounded; the breasts develop, and pubic and axillary hair appear. The fallopian tubes and uterus develop in musculature and contractility. There is increased secretion of mucous from the cervical glands, the epithelium of the vagina thickens and becomes cornified, and menstruation begins.

What causes the initiation of the changes at puberty and the release of the gonadotrophins in appreciable amounts is still a matter of considerable doubt. At least in the female, it is thought that the rise in circulating oestrogen activates a 'negative feedback controller' in the anterior hypothalamus which in turn promotes release of G T H, thence ovulation and eventually menstruation (see Donovan, 1970).

3 The Process of Sexual Differentiation

How does sexual differentiation occur?

The process of sexual differentiation is essentially the same in all mammals. This process, therefore, can be studied in detail and with relative ease, using a number of different species as experimental animals. In practice, the animal most commonly used is the laboratory rat, and for this reason, extensive reference will be made to the results of a number of experiments on these animals.

Although there are very many differences between males and females, there are four sets of characteristic features distinguishing the two sexes in mammals about which there is generally little doubt. First, there are the *gonads* – testes in males and ovaries in females. Secondly, there are the internal structures and *reproductive tracts*; thirdly, the *external genitalia*, and fourthly, the presence of an *oestrous cycle* in adult females and the absence of it in adult males.

The oestrous cycle corresponds to the cyclic release of FSH and LH. During oestrous, which occurs at ovulation, the female is sexually receptive, LH and progesterone are released and there is some vaginal discharge. Humans and some primates have a menstrual cycle where maximal receptivity and ovulation occur mid-way between the periods of bleeding.

The male has no such cycle and the release of male gonadal hormones, as well as of the gonadotrophic hormones, occurs at a fairly constant level. This cyclicity and acyclicity respectively are governed by the brain, since this is where the sequence of hormonal messages originate. This means of course that certain parts of the brain are functioning differently in males and females. The question that confronted the early workers in this field was how such differentiation according to sex, both of the brain and the accessory organs, took place – and when.

Animal experiments

The natural phenomenon of the 'freemartin' has been known for many hundreds of years. This was the name given to the abnormal calf of a twin pregnancy, the abnormality consisting of hermaphroditic sexual features. The freemartin was always the genetically female member of a twin-pair of different sexes which appeared masculinized. In such pregnancies the placentae of the foetuses were linked by connections in the blood supplies. It was deduced, naturally, that the hormones from the male were affecting and masculinizing the female.

This phenomenon was one that suggested to workers at the beginning of this century that differentiation of the reproductive tract, of the genitalia and perhaps of the brain too, were predominantly under the control of the male gonadal hormone. A number of experiments and investigations very quickly showed that the reproductive tracts and external genitalia differentiated early in development and according to whether an ovary or testis was present (Jost, 1953, 1960). The embryonic antecedents of the female reproductive structures are the mullerian ducts, and those of the male the wolffian ducts. In mammalian embryos, initially, both sets of ducts are present. The primitive embryonic ovotestis becomes an ovary or a testis, depending on the genetic message. Once a testis is formed, its secretions promote further development of the wolffian ducts to become the vas deferens, epididymis, seminal vesicles and prostate while at the same time inducing regression of the mullerian ducts. Conversely, if the primitive ovotestis becomes an ovary the mullerian ducts develop into the fallopian tubes, the uterus and vagina, while the wolffian ducts regress. But most surprising, however, is the fact that if no gonads are present, the mullerian ducts still develop and form the female type of reproductive tract. It seems that the basic mammalian propensity is to form a female, or to parody an Orwellian epigram, 'All men are born females but some are more female than others'!

Unequivocal evidence that the *brain* has differentiated in a characteristically male or female manner is only provided in adulthood, when the female individual has an oestrous or menstrual cycle. A number of experiments have been carried out to find out how and when the brain centres become sexually differentiated (Harris and Levine, 1965; Levine, 1966). Many of these experiments have used transplantation techniques: if the ovaries of a female rat and the testes of a male are removed at birth, and both given ovarian transplants when adult, they would each show normal oestrous cycles; if the testes of the male were not removed but simply moved to another part of the body, the ovarian transplant would be ineffective. These results suggested first, that in the presence of both male and female gonads, a male pattern develops, indicating a more potent role for the testicular hormone, and secondly, that the time during which the brain becomes sexually differentiated is early infancy in the rat, since the newborn rat is sexually undifferentiated. Subsequent experiments have confirmed that this process occurs in the first three to four days after birth (Harris, 1970). The potency of the testis has also been affirmed by experiments in which a testis has been implanted at birth into an intact female with the result that a *male* pattern of functioning develops. The results of these transplantation experiments can also be obtained by injecting infant animals with the appropriate hormones, or by injecting pregnant mothers in the case of guinea pigs and primates (Gerall, 1963; Young, 1965; Goy, 1968; Whalen, 1968).

The process of differentiation

It is now quite clear that during a critical period in development the secretion of the male gonad organizes first the reproductive tract and structures and then the brain according to a male pattern. It seems that nature has been remarkably provident in not permitting a neuter sex, for in the event of failure of masculine development in this period, a female will result. This is so, both in the absence of gonads as in the castrated male, and in the absence of testicular hormone due to some deficiency. This critical period varies from one species to another – immediately postnatally in rats and mice, during uterine development in rabbits and guinea pigs, and in the first trimester of pregnancy in humans – but it always occurs very early in development.

Originally it was thought that the part of the brain that was differentiated so as to regulate the hormonal patterns characteristic of males and females was the anterior pituitary gland. Experiments were then carried out which involved the transplantation of the pituitary gland from male to female rats and vice versa (Harris and Jacobsohn, 1952). The results showed that the pituitary gland functioned in accordance with the sex of the animal into which it was transplanted rather than with the sex from which it was taken, and established that the pituitary gland itself was neutral as to sex. Clearly then, sexual organization occurs one step further back – at the chief administrative organ, the hypothalamus.

This finding is particularly significant in view of the fact that the hypothalamus is also the part of the brain which is concerned with the control of behaviours which serve our basic biological needs – with eating and drinking, with motivation and with the emotions. There is recent evidence to show that cells of certain areas of the hypothalamus, notably the preoptic area, are larger in females than in males, and that the neural connections in this area are different in the two sexes (Raisman and Field, 1971). Moreover, certain of these hypothalamic areas are differentially sensitive to oestrogens and to androgens (Michael, 1962; Lisk, 1962). Because the hypothalamus is such an important control centre and because many parts of the subcortical brain are intimately connected with each other, it is unlikely that other non-sexual functions controlled by the hypothalamus remain entirely unaffected by its differentiation according to sex. Sex differences in non-sexual behaviour will, in fact, be the topic of discussion in much of the rest of the book.

To recapitulate, in the process of sexual differentiation, the

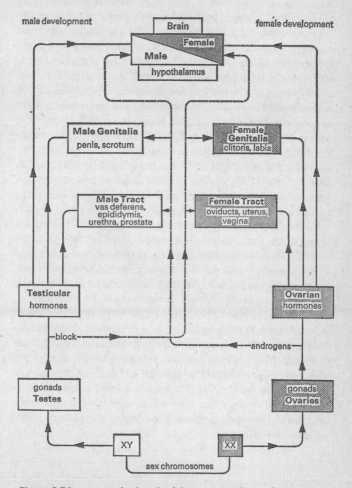

Figure 6 Diagrammatic sketch of the process of sexual differentiation in male and female. The sequence of events is read from bottom to top. By and large, presence or absence of testicular hormones in a genetic female and male respectively, pushes differentiation in the opposite direction

presence of the Y-chromosome in the fertilized egg determines 'maleness' of the foetus. It causes the medulla or inner part of the primitive gonad to develop into a testis. As soon as the ovary or testis is formed, secretion of the gonadal hormones occurs. The testicular hormone first, acting locally, organizes the primitive ducts into the male reproductive tract. (The local action of the testicular hormone is well demonstrated by the substitution of a testis for one ovary in a newborn rat: a female tract will develop on the side of the ovary and a male one on the side of the testis.) Next, the external genitalia typical of each sex develop. Finally, when the blood vessels are formed and vascular transportation is adequate, the testicular hormone acts upon the brain to differentiate it as male or female. We see that at every stage of sexual development nature has made provision that, in the event of a male not being formed, a female will result (see Figure 6).

In the development of the human embryo, for the first six weeks after fertilization, both sexes develop in the same manner. Then the testis develops and if this fails to happen, the ovary begins to differentiate a week later. At about eight weeks the ducts begin to develop into male or female structures. At every stage male differentiation *precedes* the female, the disparity increasing with time, so that by the time sexual differentiation is complete there is a four-week discrepancy: male differentiation is completed at sixteen weeks and female at twenty weeks. From external appearances the sex of the foetus is only evident after the third month of pregnancy. However, despite the fact that sexual differentiation is completed earlier in the male, in all other aspects of development the male is considerably retarded in comparison to the female, as we shall shortly see.

4 Sexual and Non-Sexual Behaviour

In most species the adult male and female can be clearly distinguished from each other in their appearance and behavioural features. Such species are described as sexually dimorphic. The dimorphism refers to characters other than the sexual organs — to plumage in birds of paradise, peacocks or bower-birds, to the size and noise of sea-elephants or fur-seals, to the songs of the canary or the chaffinch, to the mane and roar of the lion, the howl of the hyena and the antlers of the stag. In most cases it is the male which is the physically larger, more resplendent and more dominant sex. In such species the male generally makes use of the conspicuous features of his appearance or apparatus (as in song) in displays. Wynne-Edwards (1962) has referred to such ritualized or conventionalized patterns of movement, expressions or signals as *epidiectic* displays, i.e. having the function of indicating territory and ownership, dispersing potential competitors, and ultimately of controlling population density. In the animal kingdom, therefore, the role of dispersal and regulation enacted through symbolic displays and rituals is generally performed by the male.

Sexual dimorphism

There are of course many species where male and female are not readily distinguishable from each other, e.g. sparrows, geese, gibbons. But such species, at least among birds – as Wynne-Edwards points out – are nest-site rather than territorial species, and therefore, division of labour and distinction of roles between the sexes is minimal. In such cases both sexes participate in social competition as well as in care of the young. Of gibbons for example, George Schaller says:

The male and female are equal in teaching, co-ordinating, and guarding the group, and they are about equally aggressive, fighting occasionally by biting with their canine teeth and by clawing with their fingers. Gibbons show no striking sex differences in dominance (1965).

More recent evidence, however, suggests that the male gibbon takes a more active part in defending territory and in threat displays.

Although there are some species that do not distinguish very clearly between male and female, it is only very infrequently that one comes across a species in which the sex roles are reversed, that is, where the female is larger, more adorned and more aggressive than the male. Apart from the phalaropes, where reversed sex roles are manifest in three species, this phenomenon occurs only occasionally and in isolated species. According to Wynne-Edwards, this fact suggests that

... the evolution of a dominant female sex is invariably something of quite recent origin, and, by inference, therefore a 'wrong turning' or side-track likely to end in extinction (1962).

Wynne-Edwards argues that the fundamental difference between the sexes lies in the primary reproductive function of each with the result that even secondary sexual functions cannot be freely interchanged.

The underlying factor is the great difference in size, motility and cost between spermatozoa and ova. The former can be produced in millions with relatively little drain on the resources of the body, whereas the latter tend to be loaded with valuable nutrients, and consequently to be far less expendable and greatly restricted in number. Copulation has been evolved over and over again in different animal groups for the primary purpose of securing a high fertilization rate and reducing wastage of precious ova. The basic difference arises from the need for two gametes to unite their nuclei in sexual reproduction. Instead of both being alike, as they no doubt were in the beginning, the female gamete (in the metazoa) always provides the nutrients required for embryonic development and as a consequence sacrifices its mobility; whereas the male gamete is stripped down to the essential nucleus and the locomotive apparatus required in searching for the passive partner. In copulation, therefore, the motile sperms are almost always passed into the female, rather than the eggs being passed into the male (1962).

Thus, though there may be some advantage in male polygamy – since a single male may fertilize the ova of many females – there is none in female polygamy, as in principle one male is able to fertilize all her ova.

Hormonal control of sexual behaviour

Specialization in particular reproductive functions has necessitated that the female bears and succours the embryo or broods the eggs, and nurtures and protects the young, while the male fends off intruders, obtains food, and plays an active part in dispersal of the population. The male's rivalry is predominantly with other males to whom he displays in some manner and with whom he maintains some relationship within a hierarchical system. For the purpose of both epidiectic displays (which are primarily directed towards other males) as well as epigamic displays (courtship or prenuptial rituals directed at females) the male has usually developed some adornment, embellishment or accessory structures. Accompanying these morphological features are patterns of behaviour which are therefore characteristic of a particular sex. If these patterns of behaviour are directly concerned with mating they are referred to as sexual behaviours.

We are now concerned with the hormonal control of both sexual and non-sexual behaviours, particularly in mammals. During copulation, the males of most mammalian species mount the females, display pelvic thrusting and finally achieve intromission and ejaculation. Mounting, however, is also commonly shown by the female, particularly if she is on heat, and is most often directed towards another animal on heat. In many cases however the female pattern of mounting can be easily distinguished from that of the male because of its transitory nature, because it is inappropriately oriented or because it fails to lead to any of the other components of a mating sequence.

These patterns of sexual behaviour are primarily under the control of hormone action during the critical period of sexual differentiation described in chapter 3. To a lesser extent these patterns are also dependent on the level of circulating hormones. If a male rat is castrated at birth, it functions as a female: its frequency of mounting in adulthood is reduced, and it will be unable to mate successfully with a female. Conversely, if a pregnant cat, rabbit or guinea pig is injected with testosterone over a period of days at the critical period of gestation, any genetically female young she bears will be masculinized: in adulthood these androgenized females will show more mounting than normal females, and in many cases will even display pelvic thrusting and achieve intromission, since the hypertrophied clitoris will be an incomplete but adequate phallus. Adult males of many mammalian species – rats, guinea pigs, rabbits, monkeys – will show an increased frequency of mounting if given doses of testosterone but this hormone will be ineffective with adult females.

The characteristic pattern of sexual behaviour in many female mammals is lordosis, a particular form of crouching which indicates to the male that she is receptive. In general, the female displays this behaviour only during oestrous. This behaviour, too, can be modified by hormonal action. If female guinea pigs have their ovaries removed (i.e. spayed) at birth and are subsequently treated or 'primed' with oestrogen and progesterone, they will show the oestrous behaviour of normal females. The loss of their gonads does not impair their sexual performance, particularly if they are being provided with some replacement therapy, so to speak. Incidentally, from the work of Masters and Johnson (1965) we know that the same is true of human females. If, on the other hand, pregnant guinea pigs are treated with testosterone so that any genetically female offspring are hermaphroditic at birth, and these animals are then given the female hormones, the oestrous behaviour cannot be so readily obtained (Young, 1965). In fact, they behave more like normal males, only some of which show lordosis after a protracted period of treatment with female hormones (Figure 7).

From what has been described already it is clear that there are sex-typical patterns of sexual behaviour. It is important to

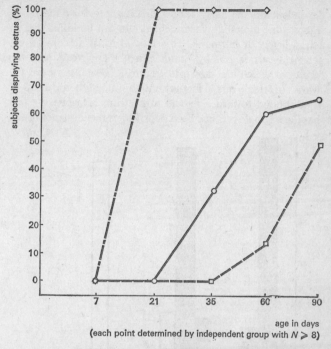

(each point determined by independent group with $N \geqslant 8$)

◇━━◇ normal females spayed at birth

○━━○ androgenized females spayed at birth.

□━━□ males castrated at birth

Figure 7 First appearance of oestrous reaction by spayed female, androgenized female, and male guinea pigs receiving oestrogen and progesterone treatment (from Young, 1965)

remember however that sexual dimorphism does not mean that certain characteristics or behaviours are *exclusively* the property of one sex, but simply that they are more *typical* of one sex than the other. Thus, certain elements of sexual behaviour like mounting or lordosis, may be shown by either sex, but in general they are shown more frequently, more definitively and more completely by one sex than the other. It is evident too that the more dimorphic of these behaviours is dependent on the early sexual differentiation of the brain, whereas the more equivocal behaviours can be influenced by actual levels of hormone. This is well illustrated in an experiment carried out by Frank Beach many years ago, the results of which are shown in Figure 8. Beach removed the ovaries of female rats in infancy and examined their behaviour in adulthood toward a female in oestrous. Despite the fact that these female rats had been deprived of the influence of *any*

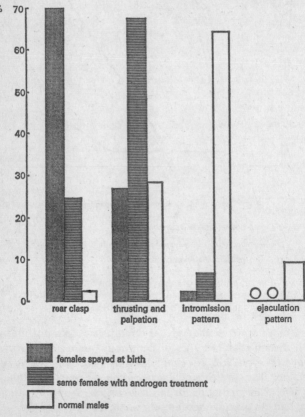

Figure 8 Relative frequency of different types of mounting responses shown by female and male rats (from Beach, 1942)

gonadal hormone during their development, they showed repeated but inadequate attempts to mount the oestrous female. (It is now known that there are particular pheromones, external hormones, secreted during oestrous to which other members of the species are particularly sensitive.) Beach found that if these spayed females were treated with androgens and then exposed to an oestrous female, they behaved more like males; mounting was more successful and many animals also displayed pelvic thrusting. The complete sequence of the male's sexual pattern, however, was impossible for these pseudo-males: as one can see from the Figure, even though androgen priming influenced the earlier elements in the sequence, intromission and ejaculation were virtually absent. The other side of the picture has been provided by Harris (1964) who castrated male rats at birth and primed them with female hormones in adulthood. These animals displayed fairly convincing feminine behaviour and were in fact more attractive to the males than normal females!

With respect to the evidence regarding the control of sexual behaviour in the guinea pig, Young states:

. . . it is conclusive that when the developing female guinea pig is subjected to the influence of androgen the neural tissues mediating mating behaviour are affected in such a way that there is a suppression of the capacity to display the feminine measures of sexual behaviour, and an intensification of the capacity to display the masculine components.

This statement is essentially true of most mammals.

Hormonal control of non-sexual behaviour

In primates and especially man, the sexual preliminaries or courtship behaviours may be much more variable, even though the copulatory sequence remains essentially stereotyped. In fact, from the work of Masters and Johnson (1965) we know that the male and female patterns of sexual behaviour in man are much less distinctive than in other species. But it is not simply the sex-typical patterns of *sexual* behaviour that are of interest to us. In many ways, and particularly in man, the differences between males and females in non-sexual behaviours appear to be more interesting and informative. Here again, much reference will be made to animal work since in these experiments the hormonal control can be more rigorously elucidated than it ever can be in man.

In most rodents, for example, females show a period of intense physical activity immediately before oestrous. This activity is well demonstrated by the persistence with which they will tread an activity wheel placed in the cage. Female rodents, being less fearful than the males, also explore an open environment or maze more actively than males, who are more inhibited in such a situation.

But primates show a greater variety in their behavioural repertoire and hence sex differences can be demonstrated more dramatically. Most of the systematic work in this respect has been done on the rhesus monkey by Harlow (1965). Harlow's

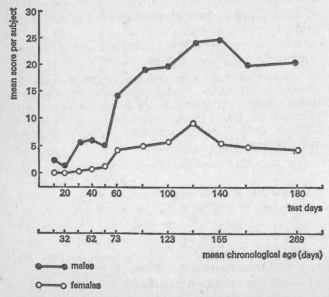

Figure 9 Development of threat responses in the playroom situation (from Harlow, 1965)

studies show that there are a number of differences between male and female infant monkeys, not only in their manner of infantile sexual posturing but in many non-sexual behaviours as well. These behaviours include the threat response (body stiffening, staring, flattening the hair on top of the head, retracting the lips and baring the teeth), passivity (sitting quietly), rigidity (a rigid body posture with averted head upon the approach of another animal) and play patterns, the most notable of them being 'rough-and-tumble' or 'contact' play consisting of wrestling, rolling and sham biting. Although in the first few weeks of life there does not seem to be much difference between the behaviour of male and female infants, presumably due to their dependency on the mother during

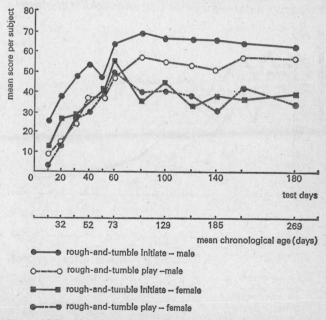

● ● rough-and-tumble initiate – male

○ ○ rough-and-tumble play – male

■ ■ rough-and-tumble initiate – female

● ● rough-and-tumble play – female

Figure 10 Development of, initiation of, and response to, rough-and-tumble play in infant monkeys (from Harlow, 1965)

this period, very soon the males show their propensity for displaying threat (Figure 9) and subsequently for initiating and engaging in rough-and-tumble play (Figure 10). The females, on the other hand, show a greater tendency for passive and anxious behaviours (Figures 11 and 12). It is tempting to explain the appearance of these sex-typical behaviours in terms of learning, imitation or some other environmentally dependent process. However, Harlow found that even if he reared infant monkeys with an inanimate surrogate mother, i.e. a wire model covered with terry-cloth, they still developed these sex-typical behaviours. That is to say, even when deprived of contact with other monkeys for much of the time, young infants, when allowed to mix together for brief periods during the day, show these characteristic patterns of behaviour: male infants after the first three weeks of life threaten

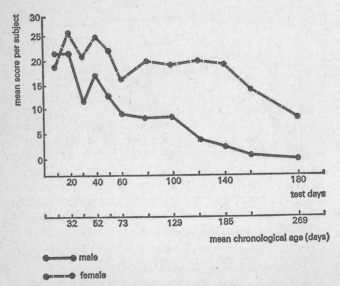

Figure 11 Manifestation of the passivity pattern by young male and female monkeys (from Harlow, 1965)

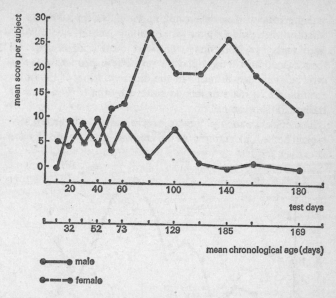

Figure 12 Development of rigidity behaviour in the playroom (from Harlow, 1965)

other animals much more frequently than do female infants (Figure 13); on the other hand, females reared in isolation show a similar tendency to passivity and rigidity. 'Rough-and-tumble' play increases during the first three months of life but is always engaged in more by male than female infants; in fact, deprivation of social experience seems to enhance the sex differences (Figure 14). The right-hand portions of these Figures show that these sex differences are consistent till well after the first year. Grooming seems to be predominantly a female activity, at least in monkey childhood (Figure 15). Of these differences Harlow said:

It is extremely difficult for us to believe that these differences are cultural, for we cannot imagine how our inanimate surrogate mothers could transmit culture to their infants.

Quite clearly then, these infant monkeys, brought up in isolation with only a dummy for company, manifested, from a fairly early age, behaviours that were more characteristic of their own than of the opposite sex. These propensities can only be explained in terms of the differentiation of the brain according to a male or female pattern by the early action of the gonadal hormones.

The evidence for the 'innate programming' of certain sex-typical behaviour patterns, as it were, was strengthened by the

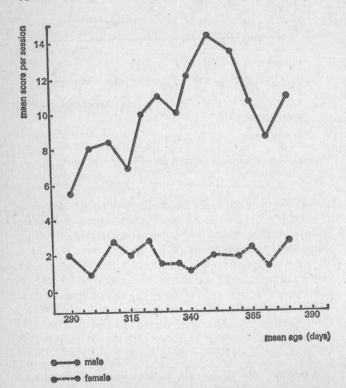

Figure 13 Sex differences in threat responses in surrogate-reared monkeys (from Harlow, 1965)

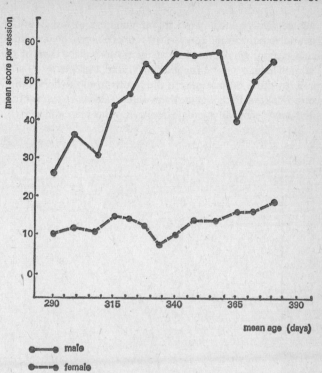

Figure 14 Sex differences in rough-and-tumble play in surrogate-reared monkeys (from Harlow, 1965)

results obtained by workers at the Department of Reproductive Physiology at the Oregon Primate Research Centre from their hermaphroditic monkeys. But first, we might consider an intriguing effect they had found earlier in the guinea pig. Male and female guinea pigs differ in the rates at which they consume oxygen in their everyday life: males consume it much more slowly than do the females. The biologists at Oregon administered testosterone to pregnant guinea pigs, thereby virilizing any female foetuses they bore. These hermaphrodite guinea pigs, genetically female but male in appearance and in neural organization, showed a *lowered* oxygen consumption rate – more similar to that of the normal male than of the normal female (Goy, Mitchell and Young, 1962).

Even more dramatic were the results from the hermaphrodite monkeys. Pregnant mothers were treated with testosterone and any genetically female foetuses were masculinized and

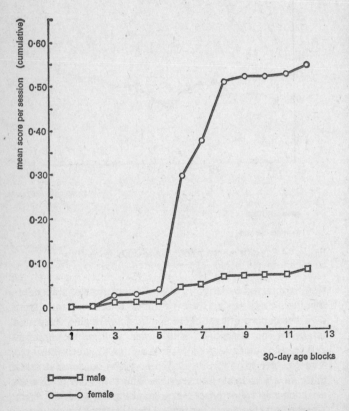

Figure 15 Development of grooming in surrogate-reared monkey infants (from Harlow, 1965)

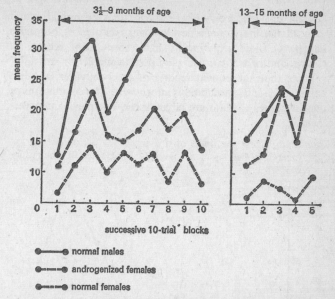

Figure 16 Frequency of rough-and-tumble play during the first and second years of life by normal male, normal female, and androgenized female (or pseudomale) rhesus monkeys (from Goy, 1968)

born as male-like hermaphrodites. Within a very few weeks of life these pseudomales were exhibiting the behaviour patterns characteristic of male infants. The frequency with which the pseudomales engaged in rough-and-tumble play for instance, was more similar to that of normal males than normal females, particularly after the first year of life (see Figure 16). Male infants, castrated on the day of birth, nevertheless continued to behave as normal males (see Figures 17 and 18). The critical period for sexual differentiation in primates being early in uterine development, the infant monkey is already anatomically and psychosexually differentiated at birth. Castration, therefore, has little effect on the functioning of centres that have already differentiated. These results from

Oregon provided conclusive evidence that hormonal action early in the individual's development has a most pervasive influence. These experiments have been fairly recent, of course, and hence data has only been available for sub-adult animals, but subsequent reports of the behaviour of these animals as adults should be as informative. The conclusions of these workers to date are circumspect, but pertinent nevertheless:

We do not know the limits of this organizing action. It may, in fact, extend to behaviors not initially anticipated as being in-

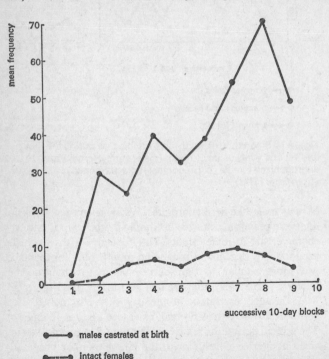

Figure 17 Frequency of threat behaviours in male rhesus monkeys castrated at birth and in normal female monkeys. Age of the animals was approximately six months (from Goy, 1968)

fluenced by hormone action. We have suspected the frequency of display of aggression and fighting in general to be related to the presence of testosterone during psychosexual development and this indirectly to dominance. ... In other areas, too, we have just begun. For example, we are investigating the role of prenatal testosterone on what may be loosely termed parental behavior. In fact, our approach to the broad problem of the organizing action of prenatal testosterone has led us to look more closely and carefully at sex differences and similarities as they exist in the untreated population (Phoenix, Goy and Resko, 1968).

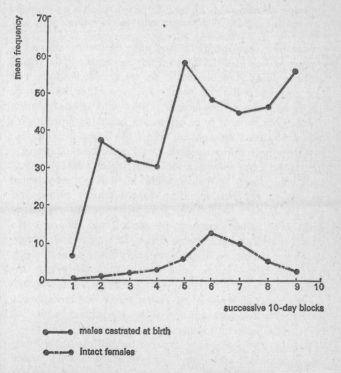

Figure 18 Frequency of rough-and-tumble play in male rhesus monkeys castrated at birth, compared with normal females (from Goy, 1968)

The guinea pig, the rhesus monkey, in fact most primates including the human, as we shall see from the findings described in the next chapter, are *not* psychosexually neutral at birth. As another Oregon worker, Robert Goy, points out:

As a result of some action of androgen on the developing nervous system, the individual, whether genetically male or female, is predisposed to the acquisition and expression of behaviors which normally characterize the genetic male. As the work progresses, the results suggest more strongly that, for a variety of mammals, early androgen influences each of those characters which is a part of the constellation of traits identifying an individual as male (1968).

Moreover, because of the sequence of events outlined in chapter 3, the dosage of hormone administered and the timing of its administration are crucial for the expected effects. For example, it would not be permissible to conclude that 'testosterone masculinizes the female'; this would be such a gross oversimplification as to be erroneous. Since the reproductive organs and tract differentiate before the brain, it is possible that there is an adequate secretion of testosterone during the former phase but not during the latter. In such a case a physical male may have an inadequately masculine psychosexual orientation or even manifest some feminine behavioural features. Conversely, a female may be exposed to a surfeit of androgens, perhaps excreted by her adrenal glands, at the stage of psychosexual differentiation, in which case she may have normal feminine features physically but be predominantly of a masculine psychological orientation. Although Goy (1968) originally noted the pertinence of such eventualities for homosexuality and other sexual anomalies, these factors are important in consideration of the development of human psychosexual identity in general.

Finally, it is worth recalling that the critical factor in the organization of the brain and neural structures is the testicular hormone, since, in its absence, a female is the inevitable result. In other words, masculine differentiation is an active process, female differentiation a passive one. Moreover, while it is relatively easy to masculinize a female animal, it is extremely difficult to feminize a male. The recent work with a androgens, for instance, shows that while the administration of substances which inhibit the action of androgen causes some feminization of a genetic male, the results are more equivocal than in the case of the androgenized female (Neumann and Elger, 1966). When human females who were virilized due to exposure to a surfeit of androgen in utero were treated with cortisone to rectify the hormonal dysfunction and surgically operated upon to restructure their genitalia, they became morphologically feminine; their behaviour and psychological orientation, however, remained essentially masculine (Ehrhardt, Epstein and Money, 1968; Money, 1970). Once 'maleness' has been stamped upon an individual it seems that its features are largely indelible.

5 Sexual Anomalies

Very often in science one learns much from one's mistakes or from an experiment which fails to yield the expected outcome. Similarly, in the study of the normal structure and function of the human or animal organism, we learn much from nature's mistakes. Such mistakes may indeed be considered 'natural experiments', since, for humanitarian or ethical reasons, it is not possible to interfere with the biological mechanisms of the individual to the extent of isolating critical factors in development.

For the purpose of our discussion, the 'errors' which have been instructive are the sexual anomalies, often referred to as the 'intersex' phenomena. In these cases, which invariably present themselves as clinical problems due to a variety of reasons, there is confusion about the sex of the individual. This confusion could arise at birth due to the ambiguous appearance of the external genitalia, during childhood due to some untoward manifestation of a secondary sex characteristic, at puberty due to failure to menstruate, or even as late as adulthood.

There are five clinical syndromes which are particularly informative: Turner's syndrome, Klinefelter's syndrome, the syndrome of testicular feminization, the adrenogenital syndrome, and progestin-induced hermaphroditism. The first two are chromosomal abnormalities, the third and fourth are endocrine dysfunctions under genetic control and the last is an endocrinological disturbance.

Turner's syndrome

In this syndrome, the individual has only forty-five chromosomes, the missing chromosome being one of the sex chromosomes. Instead of being an X Y male or an X X female, the Turner's syndrome individual is designated as X O. There are no functional gonads in such individuals and only 'streak gonads' are discernible. Nevertheless, both internal and external genitalia are clearly female, even though somewhat immaturely so. Apart from being rather small babies, individuals with Turner's syndrome may not appear at all abnormal at birth. Often, however, there are other abnormalities associated with the condition – webbed neck, loose skin, low hairline at the neck, oedema of hands or feet, or some cardio-vascular abnormality. More characteristically, the nipples are widely spaced giving the chest a shield-like appearance, and the individual is of short stature, often under five feet. This latter characteristic is certainly very obvious by the age of six or seven years and any tentative diagnosis at this time is subsequently confirmed by the failure to menstruate at puberty. These individuals are unmistakably feminine in appearance and tend to be 'ultra-feminine' in some aspects of their behaviour as we shall see shortly.

Klinefelter's syndrome

Individuals with this syndrome have an extra chromosome, their sex-chromosomal designation being X X Y. Very often there is no detectable abnormality, at least until puberty, and it is possible that a Klinefelter individual does not come to clinical notice at all. In this condition the testes are diseased and unable to produce sperm; there is also some deficiency in androgen production. But the individual is very clearly a male, though after puberty the testes may appear disproportionately small. There may also be some eunuchoid features, like elongated and slender limbs, decrease in body hair and even breast development in overweight individuals. Apart from infertility, however, there is no constantly occurring set of symptoms. As in Turner's syndrome, there may be other associated abnormalities including mental defect. There is also a loss of libido and drive; social and psychological disturbance is fairly common though the precipitating factors could be many. What is important, however, is that despite the additional X chromosome, and despite the reduced androgenic function, the individual is nevertheless indubitably male.

Testicular feminization

This is also referred to as male pseudohermaphroditism.

The term 'hermaphroditism' is reserved in humans for the condition in which both male and female gonads are present. Pseudohermaphroditism refers to the fact that the gonads are of one sex or the other but that the external appearance is of the opposite sex. Individuals with this syndrome are genetic males in whom the testes are non-functional, generally developing into an inguinal hernia. Such a person is the human analogue of the male rat castrated at birth. These cases are and remain unmistakably female: the uterus is rudimentary and the vagina is rather shallow but the external genitalia are adequately female. At puberty there is breast development but the nipples are small and the areolae very pale; there is a lack of body hair and pubic and axillary hair may be completely absent. These latter features, together with amenorrhea, are the only symptoms that are likely to provoke the individual to seek medical aid. Interestingly, the somatotype, i.e. bodily proportions and distribution of fat and muscle, of these individuals is typically feminine. Attempts have been made on occasion to modify the external genitalia by surgical intervention in accordance with the genetic sex of the individual and these 'men', despite adoption of a masculine gender identity, often continue to have a predominantly feminine orientation and to retain their female physique (Negulici, Christodirescu and Alexandru, 1968). In most cases the adults are reasonably contented *females*.

The adrenogenital syndrome

This is a case of female pseudohermaphroditism, clinically referred to frequently as congenital adrenal hyperplasia. In this condition, due to a hereditary metabolic disorder, the adrenal gland is either prevented from synthesizing cortisol, or produces a greatly reduced amount of it. Due to the nature of the hypothalamo-pituitary-adrenal loop, the low level of plasma cortisol results in stimulation of the pituitary to release increased amounts of A CT H. In the case of reduced cortisol production this additional A CT H stimulates the adrenals to discharge an adequate amount of cortisol, but it also results in the production of a surfeit of other hormones from the adrenals the release of which is also stimulated by A CT H, in particular the androgens. In the case where there is a block in cortisol synthesis, again, there is increased A CT H production in an endeavour to get the adrenals to produce more cortisol, but because of the block, all that happens is that there is an excessive build-up of substances which are precursors to cortisol, and these happen to be androgenic compounds. In an individual with the adrenogenital syndrome, therefore, the final consequence, no matter what the cause, is an excess of androgen. In the male the effect is not disastrous – growth is speeded up and there may be premature puberty.

In the female, however, the excess androgens cause virilization; the degree of masculinization may be slight or considerable, depending on the particular point in the biochemical pathway at which the block occurs, which androgenic compounds are in excess, and so on. In the mildest cases there is some hypertrophy of the clitoris and slight fusion of the labia, but distinct urethral and vaginal openings; in the severest cases there is a phallus with a penile urethra opening at its tip and complete labial (scrotal) fusion. In untreated cases of this syndrome there is generally accelerated growth in childhood and the subsequent development of masculine characteristics like hirsutism, deepening of the voice, appearance of acne and later, facial hair. At puberty there is no breast development and no menstruation. The more severe cases of this female pseudohermaphroditism are almost invariably reared as males with never a query about their 'maleness'. Some may even have married and had successful sexual relationships, including coitus with ejaculation. The latter fact is particularly surprising since these pseudomales are internally still female. In other words they have ovaries, fallopian tubes and the upper part of a vagina (Federman, 1967). In terms of physical features it is primarily their external genitalia that are masculinized. This is very probably due to the time in foetal life the androgen excess occurs: the reproductive tract has usually differentiated by the tenth week but the adrenal cortex only begins to function about the twelfth week and even then may not be doing so fully. Nevertheless, in the absence of the male gonads, it is surprising that ejaculation can occur. This finding alone would suggest that the higher neural centres have much to do with the control and facilitation of typically male and female patterns of sexual behaviour. It suggests too that levels of circulating hormones greatly influence the occurrence of this behaviour. As we shall see later on, the interests and attitudes of these hermaphroditic females are more masculine than feminine.

Early treatment with cortisone is often able to effect a complete regression of the virilized features, but hitherto the clinical problem has been one of timely detection.

Progestin-induced hermaphroditism

The last syndrome of interest concerns those infants whose mothers received sex-hormone treatment during pregnancy. Until very recently, women who tended to miscarry repeatedly were likely to be treated with hormones which would have the same effect as the natural hormone progesterone, in order to facilitate proper implantation of the foetus. In practice, these hormones were synthetic preparations, very often containing testosterone derivatives (which incidentally also have a progestational action). The foetus, being sensitive to hormonal action, became virilized (if female) by the androgenic substances that passed across the placenta. The result, though not very common, was an individual similar to one with the adrenogenital syndrome. Again, the degree of virilization was variable.

There are a number of other forms of sexual abnormality and hermaphroditism, but these cases are far fewer in number and, furthermore, their most germane characteristics are encompassed by one or other of the four categories already described.

Psychosexual neutrality or psychosexual differentiation at birth?

Having investigated a number of such sexually anomalous cases that attended the Endocrine Clinic of the Johns Hopkins School of Medicine in Baltimore, Money and the Hampsons (1955, 1957) were much concerned with the problem of 'gender role'. By this they meant the gender identity – male or female, boy or girl, man or woman – which the individual adopted. What these workers claimed they found was that, despite the ambiguities in sexual characteristics, many individuals nevertheless adopted, quite satisfactorily, the gender role to which they were assigned. They pointed out that the sex to which such an individual might be assigned could be contrary to any one of the several variables of sex: to the chromosomal composition, to the gonads, to the hormones, to the internal reproductive structures, or to the external genitalia. Nevertheless, with few exceptions, these individuals apparently accepted their sex of assignment and acted in accordance with it. Even reassignment to the other sex was possible, provided it was done early.

Such results led these psychiatrists to propose a theory of *psychosexual neutrality at birth*. This theory sees the human individual being sexually neuter and psychologically neutral at birth, and becoming psychosexually differentiated in the process of growing up. This neutral organism was seen as capable of being 'flipped' to the masculine or 'flopped' to the feminine identity, as the need arose. But it was important that gender identity be established by the age of three years, since it was during the first two or three years that the child, through a process very similar to imprinting, acquired the behaviour patterns, interests, attitudes and proclivities appropriate to its sex. This theory of psychosexual neutrality, with its strongly environmental and cultural bias, has dominated the study of sex differences in the United States to such an extent that psychologists consistently use the jargon terms 'sex typing', 'sex role identification', 'sex role adoption' in discussions of sex differences in human behaviour, these terms implying that there is considerable choice in the matter. The observations of Money and the Hampsons simply strengthened the prevailing empiricist view that 'boys are boys and girls are girls because they are reared that way, not because they are born that way'.

This is a view I strongly dispute. Money and the Hampsons did invaluable work in bringing the problems of gender identity under closer scrutiny than they had previously received and in urging consideration of several factors before deciding upon gender assignation. With their conclusions, however, I simply cannot agree. My contention rests on several grounds.

First, in over 99 per cent of human beings there is little doubt about the sex of an individual. Its sex is as important to an individual's identity as whether it is alive. A perspicuous psychologist remarked many years ago: 'Persons do not exist; there are only male persons and female persons – biologically, sociologically and psychologically' (Colley, 1959). The fact that very infrequently a case of sexual ambiguity presents itself is regrettable, is even instructive, but does nothing to alter the fact that in general it is males and females that are born.

Secondly, the Money and Hampson argument is specious. Any incongruity between the sex of assignment on the one hand and the chromosomal, gonadal or reproductive features on the other is irrelevant. For, in the normal process of differentiation the chromosomal constitution determines the gonads that develop, and the hormones secreted from these in turn determine the nature of the tract and the external genitalia, but when there has been an aberration in some part of the sequence, the elements antecedent to that point are no longer relevant in the same manner. In other words, given an interruption of the normal sequence of events, the critical factor becomes the exposure, or not, to androgenic influences.

Thirdly, at the moment of birth, the sex of the infant is ascertained from the appearance of the genital organs. It cannot be otherwise. If there really is some confusion, there might be recourse to sex-chromatin investigations, but the validity of this procedure in such instances is extremely doubtful. In cases of pseudohermaphroditism, the more masculinized the genital features, the more likely is the sex assignment to be male and the more likely is the brain itself to have been organized in a masculine pattern under the influence of the androgens. On the other hand if the external genitalia are only minimally virilized, the chances are that the individual will be assigned to the female sex and androgenic influence upon neural organization would have been slight, hence the individual will tend to be more feminine than masculine. Reference to chromosomal or gonadal sex in such cases is therefore beside the point. This fact is well illustrated by two of Money's own cases of the adrenogenital syndrome. One was 'diagnosed' as a girl, the other 'misdiagnosed' as a male hermaphrodite. Both cases were given surgical treatment in accordance with the diagnoses; cortisone was also administered. At puberty the individuals appeared as in Figure 19. Money uses these cases as illustrations of the degree of 'developmental pliability' possible after birth, thereby begging the question of *why* different procedures should have been carried out on the two cases. The bases for these respective diagnoses were surely differences in external appearance?

Finally, the fact that few of these hermaphrodites repudiate their assigned gender role does not necessarily mean that the individuals are satisfied or at ease with this role; nor does it mean that the behaviour, the attitudes, the interests of such individuals are in accordance with the role. To repudiate one's sex is tantamount to repudiating one's identity. To adopt a different gender role, therefore, is to adopt a new identity – a drastic course of action that could only be provoked by the most refractory disturbance and compounded of many features – physical, behavioural, emotional and sexual. The small number of individuals who change their gender role, dubious though it be, should occasion little surprise. It is certainly *not* evidence that the human organism at birth is so malleable that it can be pushed psychosexually left or right with impunity. Moreover, the fact that an individual adopts one gender role or the other does not imply that he or she does so with equanimity. Nor does it tell one how the person acts out that role. It is quite conceivable than an individual who has been assigned, and has adopted, the female gender role, may

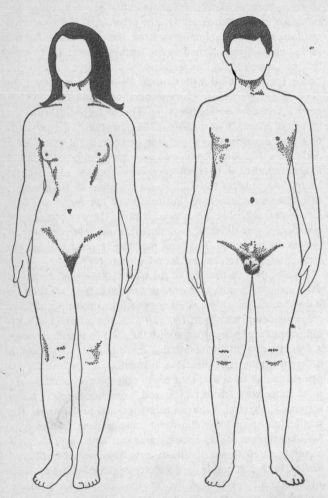

Figure 19 Two patients with the adrenogenital syndrome of female hermaphroditism : both are genetic females but one is reared as a girl and the other as a boy (diagram from Money and Ehrhardt, 1968)

nevertheless have boyish interests and in many ways behave more like a male than a female, and vice versa, of course. The strongest evidence in support of such a likelihood has recently been provided by Money himself.

Money and Ehrhardt (1968) compared a group of genetically female patients with adrenogenital hermaphroditism and a group with progestin-induced hermaphroditism with a group of patients with Turner's syndrome. The comparisons therefore were between androgenized females and 'females' exposed to no sex hormonal influences at all but who, by many criteria, seemed excessively feminine. The age of patients in all three groups ranged from early childhood to late adolescence. These comparisons were concerned primarily with patterns of behaviour, attitudes and interests, and were most illuminating (Figure 20). Whereas none of the patients with Turner's syndrome showed 'intense outdoor physical and athletic interests' all but one of the androgenized females did so; whereas none of the Turner cases regarded themselves or were considered by others to be a tomboy, most of the hermaphroditic cases did, and were also regarded so by others. The majority of the androgenized girls preferred boys' toys to girls' toys, some of them playing *only* with boys' toys, while all the Turner girls preferred girls' toys to boys'. The same was true of clothes. No androgenized girls put marriage before a career, some put a career before marriage and many wanted both; of the girls with Turner's syndrome some put marriage before a career, more wanted both, but only one put a career before marriage and she wished to be a nun! Psychologists and psychiatrists often use a test called the Draw-a-Person test as a diagnostic tool in enabling them to obtain indications about an individual's maturity, psychosexual identification and similar traits. In performing this test every one of the Turner's females depicted their own sex first, only 64 per cent of the others did so. These differences in behaviour and interests between the somewhat masculinized females and the 'hyperfemales' seems fairly convincing evidence that many of our everyday activities and interests are at least partly a function of our early hormonal experience.

The sexual anomalies, nature's errors in genetic and hormonal programming, have provided us with invaluable information regarding some of the least explicit mechanisms in human development. Despite Hampson's assertion that

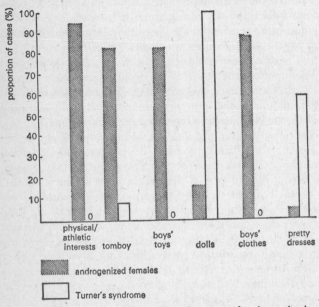

Figure 20 The interests and activities of a group of androgenized females compared with those of a group of Turner's syndrome cases. All individuals have been reared as females (data from Money and Ehrhardt, 1968)

'psychologic sex or gender role appears to be learned, that is to say, it is differentiated through learning during the course of the many experiences of growing up' (1965) the evidence to date has made such a view untenable by the demonstration that any form of sexual neutrality does not exist in the human species, nor indeed in the biological kingdom. This is not to say that experiences and social influences are unimportant, but these act upon an organism that is *already biased in a male or female direction*.

Even Money appears to have grudgingly conceded this. In 1963 he wrote: 'It is more reasonable to suppose simply that, like hermaphrodites, all the human race follow the same pattern, namely, of psychosexual undifferentiation at birth.' But in 1968 he was able to say: 'There may well be a foetal hormonal effect on subsequent psychosexual differentiation ... (which) bestows a special quality on behavioural development as a female.'

The greater cerebral development of man has indeed given him a wider range of options than those available to other mammalian species and a greater degree of independence in his exercise of them. To assume that all these are equiprobable is contrary to the evidence and to the laws of biology.

6 Boys and Girls

In the cultural climate of the present, it is considered foolish or intrepid to refer to sex differences in our own species – differences which are pervasive and which are manifest in biological, psychological and social functions. Whether we like it or not, *homo sapiens* too is a sexually dimorphic species, and it may be as well to remember that in many ways the sexual dimorphism is more pronounced in humans than in many other primates:

... humans are rather more dimorphic in body-mass than chimpanzees, and much more dimorphic than any other hominoid in the development of epigamic characters, especially on the breast and about the head and neck, which can only be paralleled, in primates, in some baboons. Equally, there seems little to suggest that human males are any less competitive and aggressive among themselves than those of other species; the difference rather lies in the fact that these attributes are expressed in culturally-determined channels ... rather than by species-specific threat gestures or physical assault, so that expression of rage is postponed and channelled, not abolished at source (Jolly, 1970).

In fact, distinctively male and female development in the human being begins at the moment of conception. There being only one X-chromosome in the male, all X-borne genes will be manifest, even recessive ones, whereas the female will be a 'functional mosaic' of X-borne genes (Hunt, 1966) due to the inactivation of one X-chromosome in each cell, as we saw in chapter 1. The evidence considered in that chapter showed that from very early in uterine life males are more vulnerable to all manner of accidents and insults. Even adverse conditions like dietary deficiencies affect boys more severely than they do girls. The increased risk to men of disease and accident cannot be attributed to occupational stresses, since comparisons of religious communities into which priests and nuns had been initiated early in life, thereafter living very similar lives, reveals that again the women outlive the men. It seems that brevity of the life-span is generally inherent in the masculinity of the individual. According to the Vital Statistics of the United States, 1962, if you are a woman of thirty years, you can expect to live another forty-seven years, but if you are a man of thirty you can only hope to survive another forty-one years (Scheinfeld, 1965).

The fact that in many species more males than females are conceived is nature's way of ensuring an adequate number of surviving males. The manner in which this occurs is not absolutely clear as yet but there is a suggestion that the Y-chromosome-bearing sperm is more speedy than the X-bearing sperm and hence reaches the ovum first.

Growth and maturation

At birth male infants are both heavier and longer than females. In fact, even *in utero* the male grows faster than the female and continues to do so, although with progressive deceleration, until about seven months after birth, after which the girl grows faster until about four years. The average girl is both shorter and lighter than the average boy of the same age until eight years or so (Tanner, 1970).

The calorie intake of boys exceeds that of girls from the second month onwards. Even in childhood the calcium levels in boys are higher and after puberty their potassium needs too are greater. From infancy to senescence males have a consistently higher basal metabolism, they develop proportionally larger hearts and lungs, and have a greater vital capacity. Even at birth, girls have more fat than boys, and whereas in adolescence and thereafter they show an increase in subcutaneous fat particularly in the trunk region, boys actually lose fat in adolescence. On the other hand, from infancy to adulthood boys have larger and stronger muscles than girls (Jones, 1949). This can be seen clearly in Figure 21, where the graphs represent the force with which the arms are pulled apart when the hands are clasped in front of the chest, and conversely, the force with which they are pushed apart. Whereas boys continue to develop in strength even after puberty, girls seem to reach a plateau, and at a much lower level. The differences in dietary intake and demands, in enzyme efficiency and metabolism, must also be inevitably reflected in behavioural differences during childhood.

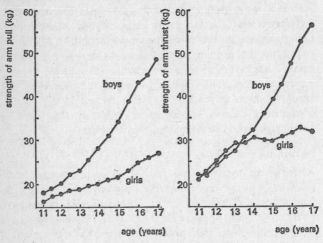

Figure 21 Strength of arm-pull and arm-thrust from age eleven to seventeen. Mixed longitudinal data, 65–93 boys and 66–93 girls in each group (from Tanner, 1970)

A significant difference between the sexes, as pointed out in chapter 2, is that the male hormone facilitates protein synthesis while the female hormones have no such action. It is interesting that during the war the United States Department of Agriculture suggested that the protein allowance per day should be seventy grams for men and fifty grams for women. Boys and men have a lower resting heart-rate but a higher systolic blood pressure, which means the heart has more 'room for manoeuvre' in cases of stress or physical exertion. They are also able to carry more oxygen in the blood and have a considerable increase of haemoglobin particularly after puberty (see Figure 22). This increase in red cells is due directly to the action of the male hormone. Males are also more efficient at neutralizing metabolites like lactic acid which are the by-products of exercise and work. Thus we see that there are a number of structural and functional features which are adaptively different in boys and girls and which in general equip the male for a more active and strenuous life (Tanner, 1970). The male has also been likened to an engine operating at higher levels of speed and intensity and which therefore needs more fuel than the less energetic female.

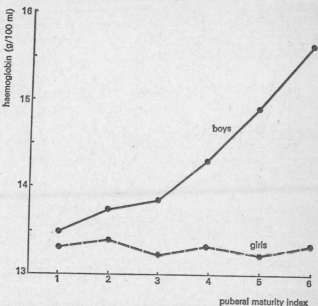

Figure 22 Blood haemoglobin level in girls and boys according to stage of puberty. Cross-sectional data (from Young, 1963)

Despite the typical male's impressive physical advantages, however, he is developmentally retarded in comparison with the female. This retardation begins early in foetal life and continues to adulthood. At twenty weeks after conception the male foetus is retarded by two weeks and at forty weeks by four weeks. The newborn girl is equivalent to the four to six-week-old boy in terms of physical maturity, i.e. as an approximation to the adult state. In growth velocity, for example, the typical boy lags about two years behind the typical girl (Figure 23). Bone ossification and dental maturity are both

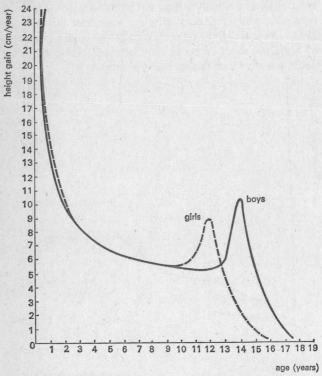

Figure 23 Typical-individual velocity curves for supine length or height in boys and girls. These curves represent the growth velocity of the typical boy and girl at any given instant (from Tanner. Whitehouse and Takaishi, 1966)

achieved earlier by girls; so is physiological maturity indicated by puberty (see Figure 24). In accordance with the greater maturity of these structural features in girls are the advances in behavioural development. Girls tend to sit up, crawl and walk before boys. They also learn to talk earlier. We shall see in later chapters that girls are more advanced and more mature in a number of skills and aptitudes.

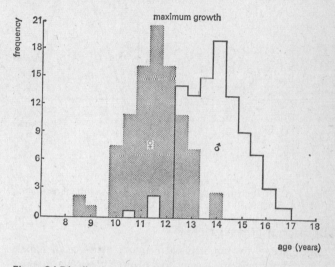

Figure 24 Distributions of boys and girls according to the age at which they achieve physical maturity (from Nicolson and Hanley, 1953)

Premenstrual syndrome

At menarche and thereafter many girls may suffer, physically and psychologically, from a variety of symptoms associated with this syndrome. The psychological symptoms usually consist of irritability, depression or lethargy, or even all of them, and seem to be due to a sodium–potassium imbalance – sodium retention within the cell and potassium depletion from it. Dalton (1969) has shown how pervasive the effects of premenstrual tension can be, and illustrates how the performance of schoolgirls may be adversely affected (see Figure 25). Awareness of such handicaps may be particularly important in evaluating the examination and test performances of adolescent girls.

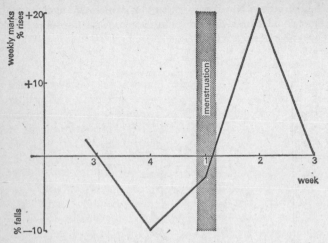

Figure 25 Variation in schoolgirls' weekly grades with menstruation (from Dalton, 1969)

Behavioural differences at birth

Male infants are not necessarily more active than female infants but they do appear to be more vigorous in their activity. During the neonatal period, i.e. the first ten days of life, infants commonly exhibit spontaneous startles, a sudden convulsive movement of the whole body, particularly when deeply asleep. In addition, boys have spontaneous penile erections, also in deep sleep. Soon after birth and for the next few days boys show these kinds of gross and vigorous bodily movements more often than girls. The movements of the girl infants on the other hand tend to be finer and more restricted ones like twitchings of the lips, smiling, sucking, or raising of the brows (Korner, 1969).

Information regarding other aspects of behaviour or feeding and sleeping patterns during the newborn period is still lacking. But by the age of three weeks boys are found to sleep less than girls; they are also more fretful and irritable. The girls appear to be more placable. More as a consequence of these behavioural differences rather than as a cause of them, mothers seem to react differently to their male and female babies: boys are looked at, stimulated, and pacified more than girls (see Hutt, 1972a).

Sensory capacities

As long ago as 1894 Francis Galton noted that women had lower touch and pain thresholds than did men. This greater sensitivity to touch and to pain is an intrinsic characteristic of the female and has been observed from the moment of birth. Females also hear better than males: their auditory discrimination and localization is superior at all ages. Males, on the other hand, see better. These sex-typical advantages in sensory capacities are not learned or acquired through particular forms of experience: they are evident in infancy. Even at a few weeks of age boys show more interest in visual patterns, while infant girls attend more to tonal sequences. Differences in sensitivity mean that males and females are likely to respond differently to the same stimuli (Kagan, 1969). In his memorable report, Kinsey commented on the greater susceptibility of the adult male to visually erotic stimuli. The sensitivity first evident in the cradle is amply exploited by the strip-teaser and pornographer. Money (1963) himself remarked that, 'In general, men are more readily responsive than are women to visual and narrative material, women being dependent on tactile stimulation', and conceded that the evidence from the pseudohermaphrodites would suggest that these sensory proclivities are dependent on the early organizing action of androgen. These sex-dependent characteristics are not unique to our species – they have been observed in monkeys and even in the rat (see Buffery and Grey, 1972).

A fascinating consequence of the female's greater auditory sensitivity has been reported very recently (Simner, 1971). It is well known by any nursery caretaker that the cry of a baby can start other babies crying. It seems that even at three days of age babies are more responsive to the cry of another baby than to an artificially produced sound of the same intensity, and girl babies are more responsive in this respect than boy babies.

The early dependence on different sensory channels also has the consequence that the same stimuli have a different *significance* for boys and girls, and men and women. Watson (1969) demonstrated this quite dramatically when he attempted to condition an operant response in fourteen-week-old infants. In the process of operant conditioning some motor response has to be performed, often inadvertently, in the presence of a 'neutral' stimulus, a stimulus which is not associated with fear or appetite of any kind. By rewarding or reinforcing this response each time it is performed in the presence of the stimulus, it becomes a conditioned response to that stimulus, and thenceforth it is reliably performed whenever that stimulus appears. Watson simply wanted to condition the babies to 'look at' a spot of light whenever it appeared. The remarkable fact was that he was only able to do so successfully if he used sounds as reinforcement for the girls and lights as reinforcement for the boys. The training was unsuccessful if he used visual reinforcement for the girls and auditory reinforcement for the boys. This was one of the first systematic demonstrations of the importance of stimulus *salience* in the processes of early human learning.

The adaptive significance of these particular sensitivities will be discussed in the final chapter.

Cerebral asymmetry

In man, the right and left cerebral hemispheres control rather different functions: the right hemisphere is more involved in the control of perceptual-motor, spatial, and non-verbal functions, whereas the left hemisphere is predominantly concerned with language functions. This lateralization of function at least applies to most right-handed people. In dichotic listening experiments, where a subject is required to repeat what he hears when different stimuli are simultaneously presented to the two ears, the stimuli to the *right* ear are reported more accurately if the two sets of stimuli are spoken series of digits. This finding is interpreted in terms of the greater efficiency of the left hemisphere in dealing with verbal signals. Since the left hemisphere receives input from the contralateral ear, i.e. the right, it is these stimuli which are preferentially recalled (Kimura, 1961). If, however, the stimuli presented are non-verbal ones like musical melodies, then the ones presented to the *left* ear are recalled better (Kimura, 1964), demonstrating that such input is primarily dealt with by the right hemisphere. Such lateralization in dealing with verbal input like spoken digits was found for girls but not for boys at the age of five years (Kimura, 1963). Even more interesting, when the stimuli are non-verbal noises and animal sounds, boys of this age are more accurate at recalling the stimuli presented to the left ear (and hence dealt with by the right hemisphere) than are girls. These results suggested to Knox and Kimura (1970) that the right hemisphere functions rather differently in the two sexes.

Reviewing an impressive volume of literature of this kind relating to the neural mechanisms subserving linguistic and non-linguistic functions, Buffery and Gray (1972) propose that there is an innate neural mechanism for speech perception. They suggest that this mechanism is more developed in the female than in the male brain of the same age, with the consequence that the lateralization of linguistic functions to the left hemisphere is accelerated in the female. They also suggest that in the male this lateralization of verbal function is less complete than in the female. If this were so, it would mean that there were 'unused' neural structures in the left hemisphere of the male – structures which would have been pre-empted by language in the female. These 'available' structures in the left hemisphere would permit a more bilateral, but still largely right-sided, representation for non-verbal functions in the male. These authors imply that a more bilateral control also means a more efficient control, hence the male superiority in spatial functions. What is somewhat paradoxical however is that on the one hand greater lateralization is seen to account for the superior verbal ability of the female but a more *bilateral* representation to account for the superior spatial ability of the male. Nevertheless, there is tentative support for structural differences subserving these lateralized functions: upon conducting histopathological analyses of the brains of children

Conel (1963) found that, at the age of four years, myelination and dendritic growth in certain areas was greater in the left hemisphere of girls and in the right hemisphere of boys. This finding might be interpreted as evidence of greater functional activity in these hemispheres at this age.

Finally, an unexpected finding from clinical data adds weight to the evidence in favour of sex differences in structural and functional cerebral asymmetry. On examining the records of children who had developed febrile convulsions in infancy and early childhood, Taylor (1969) found that if the fever had occurred before the age of two years, a lesion was more likely to occur in the left hemisphere, but after the age of two years it was likely to occur in the right. In other words, in infancy the left hemisphere was more vulnerable. On the principle of a functionally active organ being less at risk to an insult, Taylor argued that early in life it is the *right* hemisphere which is functional, being concerned with the development of control of perceptual-motor abilities, and hence less vulnerable; after the age of two it is the *left* hemisphere which is more active in the development and organization of linguistic abilities. Thus, the left hemisphere is at risk only until it begins to be involved in the control of language. Taylor found that this period of risk to the left hemisphere was shorter in girls than in boys and interpreted this, quite reasonably, as evidence that the female brain matures more rapidly than, and lateralizes function in advance of, the male brain.

In summary, it is possible to say that the evidence to date, though not conclusive, is strongly suggestive that the structural and functional organization of human male and female brains is different from a very early age, and possibly from the time of sexual differentiation.

7 Intelligence and Special Abilities

Intelligence

Are men more intelligent than women? This indeed is a
perennial chestnut for psychologists. Perhaps a word should
be said first about what we mean by intelligence. To a
certain extent, intelligence is what intelligence tests measure,
but this statement is not as tautologous as it may seem.
It is simply easier to describe what intelligence tests are
measuring than to enter into debate about what constitutes
intelligence.

Basically, there are two forms of measurable intelligence:
verbal and non-verbal. Verbal intelligence is measured in
terms of vocabulary, general knowledge, ability to comprehend
verbally presented situations, and to form class concepts;
logical reasoning is tapped indirectly since a lack of it mani-
fests itself in both verbal and non-verbal tests. Non-verbal
intelligence is measured in terms of a number of performances
many of which are timed, since it is not the ability to do the
task *per se* that is important but the speed with which it is
done. The ability to assemble the component parts of a figure,
to arrange a number of patterned blocks according to a two-
dimensional figure, to substitute a code, are some of the
abilities which constitute a performance or non-verbal I Q.
In general, there is little discrepancy between verbal and
performance I Qs, and the total I Q is an average of these two
measures. There are certain discrepancies which are to be
expected: for instance, most people who have had a grammar-
school education tend to have a higher verbal than performance
I Q; apprentices, students in technical streams or colleges, and
children from the lower socioeconomic classes more often tend
to have a higher performance than verbal I Q.

Similarly, because of the particular aptitudes of males and females, the patterns of their scores on the different tests are appreciably different. For example, girls and women tend to score higher on the verbal tests and nearly always do better than boys and men on the coding test which calls for short-term memory, speed and deftness; the males, on the other hand, invariably achieve higher scores on arithmetic and on block-design, the visuo-spatial test. Thus, although there is little evidence that men and women differ in *average* intelligence, the constitution of intelligence in the two sexes is far from similar.

This fact was well illustrated in the development of one of the most widely used tests of intelligence, the Wechsler Adult Intelligence Scale (WAIS). In the course of the construction and standardization of such a test, an attempt is made to exclude those items which appear to penalize some section of the population for reasons ostensibly unrelated to ability. Hence in the original WAIS, constructed in 1931, Wechsler discarded those items on which the sexes performed very differently. Despite this, sex differences continued to appear and in 1958, introducing a second edition of his test, Wechsler conceded that:

Our findings do confirm what poets and novelists have often asserted, and the average layman long believed, that men not only behave but *think* differently from women.

It is precisely for the reason that individuals differ in the pattern of their abilities that one or other of these test scores would be a misleading estimate of general intelligence. It is for this reason, too, that psychologists often have reservations about quoting an I Q figure, since it can reflect a wide scatter in abilities or a very consistent performance. It certainly is not permissible to interpret, as some workers have done, the linguistic superiority of women as evidence of their mental superiority. Moreover, because of their advanced maturity in general, and their precocity in language development in particular, girls will be at an advantage on verbal tests of intelligence. It is only in late adolescence, when the abilities of boys have 'matured', so to speak, that reliable comparisons between the sexes can be made.

Even so, there seems to be little evidence that males and females differ in terms of their average ability. For instance, in 1939 the Scottish Council for Research in Education tested all children who had been born on 1 February, 1 May, 1 August and 1 November in 1926. The average I Qs were 100·51 for the boys and 99·7 for the girls, and very comparable results were obtained a decade later.

Nevertheless, the *distributions* of male and female scores are very different. In other words, if a large number of men and women are tested, the scores of the women will tend to cluster around the overall average for the whole group of women, whereas the scores of the men will spread more across

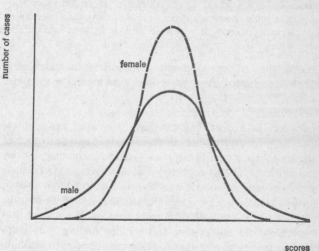

Figure 26 Theoretical distribution of intelligence for the two sexes : more males will be found amongst the very low I Qs as well as amongst the very high I Qs (from Tyler, 1965)

the range (see Figure 26). This is an expression of the law of greater variability in the male which we have already discussed in chapter 1. This appears to be true of most characteristics which can be quantitatively measured – e.g. weight, height, intelligence. It is this tendency for a more conservative expression of characteristics in females which Heim (1970) has referred to as 'The Mediocrity of Women'.

... there is a tendency for men to be 'more so' than females, whatever is being tested. Thus on intelligence tests, for instance, when groups of comparable young men and women take tests, they tend to gain mean scores which are similar, but the highest and the lowest scorers are liable to be male. This finding is not confined to intelligence tests or even to psychological tests in general. It applies also to academic examinations. There is a tendency for women students to gain proportionately more second-class degrees – and, thus, fewer first and thirds – in many examination subjects.

In the 'real world' situation, the same tendency holds: men rather than women are found at the extremes. There are more male geniuses, more male criminals, more male mental defectives, suicides and stutterers, more colour-blind males, than females. This list is a long one, with relatively few exceptions.

The fact that males predominate in the intellectual and creative echelons seems to have a basis other than masculine privilege.

Hormones and intelligence

Two sets of recent findings have provoked considerable speculation regarding the effects of early exposure to the sex hormones upon central nervous system functioning. Money and Ehrhardt (1968) reported that the average IQ of their sample of genetic females who had been exposed to androgen early in development was significantly higher than the average IQ of a control sample of normal females. The authors unfortunately did not discuss this striking finding, only commenting that early exposure to androgens appears to facilitate intellectual development.

In the same year, Dalton reported her results of children whose mothers had been treated with therapeutic doses of progesterone during the second trimester of pregnancy. Dalton's findings were that these children were significantly advanced in their early development compared with a control group of children. Many of the progesterone children passed their motor milestones earlier than the controls. This advanced development appeared to be maintained throughout childhood and an educational follow-up at the age of nine to ten years showed that the school achievements of these children were superior to those of the controls. Even more strikingly, the superiority of those children whose mothers had been on a high dose of progesterone (more than eight grams during pregnancy) was greater than those whose mothers had received a considerably lower dose. Although in large doses progesterone has an androgenic action, none of these children were at all virilized. Dalton does not proffer any explanation for her results either, results which are remarkably concordant with those of Money and Ehrhardt. One might speculate, however, that steroid hormones with an androgenic action, by their facilitative action on protein synthesis, in particular brain RNA, enhance neural integration – thus promoting more 'intelligent' behaviour. But if this were so, it is surprising that normal males and females do not differ in average I Q.

Perceptual abilities

In the last chapter we considered sex differences which exist in visual and auditory abilities. These differences are apparent from such an early age and so universally that a cultural basis for them seems unlikely. Freedman (1971) found that some of these differences can be seen in the first few days of life and in widely differing societies.

Males and females differ in a number of other sensory and perceptual capacities too. For instance, women have a keener sense of smell than men. This ability, moreover, appears to be dependent upon the circulating levels of oestrogen: women whose ovaries are under-functioning for some reason are less sensitive to smell, but if treated with oestrogen their olfactory acuity improves. The sense of smell is also poorer during menstruation when the level of oestrogen is depressed.

From birth, females are more sensitive than males to touch and to pain. Female infants at a few hours of age react more strongly to being brushed on the skin and to mild electrical stimulation (Lipsitt and Levy, 1959). In adulthood, the woman's tolerance of pain is considerably less than the man's – in general, a man will endure a higher level of painful stimulation before he declares it 'unbearable' (Notermans and Tophopf, 1967). There is a common belief that women are the stoics in this respect, but perhaps this may arise as a result of confusion between the painful experiences women habitually undergo – menstruation, childbirth etc. – and the manner in which they withstand them. On the other hand, it may be that women deal more adequately with *protracted* periods of pain or discomfort. Our expectations of boys to suffer insults and injuries manfully seem to have some physical basis. It is interesting too that disintegration of the personality, as in severe psychotic illness, does not obliterate these sex differences.

Spatial ability

Males excel in spatial ability (Guilford, 1967). The skills involved are usually referred to as visuo-spatial skills since they concern the ability to organize and relate visual inputs in their spatial context. This ability is manifest in activities as diverse as aiming at a target, arranging objects according to a two-dimensional pattern, or having a good sense of direction. Although visual acuity would help in visuo-spatial abilities, it would not wholly account for the male's advantage in these, since they principally relate to spatial relationships and orientation. Buffery and Gray find that this ability is not unique to the male sex of the human species – chimpanzees and rats share it too. It is an ability which cultural factors seem to affect hardly at all. One of its manifestations is the ability to maintain accurate spatial orientation and to detect spatial relationships despite distortions of and camouflage by the contour or background, commonly referred to as *field-independence*.

Witkin *et al.* (1962) used two well-known tests to evaluate field dependence – the Rod-and-Frame test and the Embedded-Figure test. In the former, the subject sitting in a darkened room, is required to judge the verticality of a rod against different degrees of tilt of the luminous frame (background), and in the latter the subject has to extract a particular figure from a context which both embeds it and disguises it. Men are less distracted by the misleading cues of the context and are able to perform better on these tests. This is true of a variety of very different cultures. There is evidence of male superiority in this respect as early as three or four years of age (Eckert, 1970).

There is some evidence that this ability is in part genetically determined (Stafford, 1961). If the scores of parents and children on visuo-spatial tests are compared, it is found that the correlations between mothers and sons, and between fathers and daughters, are fairly high; the correlations between the scores of mothers and daughters is considerably lower while that between fathers and sons is zero. This evidence argues for at least one of the genes controlling visuo-spatial ability being a recessive carried on the X-chromosome, and can be explained in the following manner. A sex-linked recessive gene can only be expressed in females if it is present in both X-chromosomes, but can be expressed in any male since there is no dominant counterpart in the absence of another X-chromosome. Thus, if the mother has the gene on both X-chromosomes then all sons will inevitably manifest this trait, whereas a daughter's second X-chromosome from her father may not have the gene, in which case she cannot manifest it: this accounts for the higher mother–son than mother–daughter correlation. Similarities between performances, however, can arise both from the expression of the gene as well as the failure to express it, hence there is also some correlation between mother and daughter. The father does not transmit an X-chromosome to his son and hence there is no correlation between their abilities.

There is also evidence that spatial ability develops under the control of the sex hormones, or, more precisely, that the genetic message is translated through the sex hormones. In certain cases of kwashiorkor there is an endocrine disturbance which results in feminization of the males. West African men who are feminized in this manner score lower than their normal counterparts on visuo-spatial tests and they show greater field-dependence on the Witkin tests (Dawson, 1967 a, b) than do other men.

Verbal ability

It is in the area of verbal skills that women come into their own (Tyler, 1965). Girls learn to talk earlier than boys, they articulate better and acquire a more extensive vocabulary than boys of a comparable age. In all aspects of language usage their performance is considerably superior: they write and spell better, their grammar is more competent and they are able to construct sentences more adequately. It must be remembered, however, that in many instances of particular boy-girl comparisons, such differences may be very slight. These differences only manifest themselves unambiguously in large-scale comparisons of boys and girls.

In a systematic study of the early language development in a sample of London children, Moore (1967) found that many of the differences between the boys and the girls were not statistically different but were, nevertheless, *consistently* different. Thus, although the Speech Quotient of girls was significantly higher than that of boys at eighteen months, the difference at six months or at three years was not very great. On the other hand, the Speech Quotient in girls predicted well the subsequent course of language development, even as early as six months. In the boys there was no such conformity in the pattern of linguistic development: it seemed that no measure at an early age could foretell future performance of any kind in this area. As Moore commented: 'linguistic development runs a steadier course from an earlier age in female infancy.'

Even more interesting was Moore's finding that in girls the early linguistic measures were highly predictive of later measures of intelligence. This was not so in boys who were much more erratic in their development, the most distinguished example being a three-year-old with an IQ of 78 who turned out to be a 'genius' with an IQ of 151 at eight. The conclusion to be drawn from Moore's study is that intellectual development in girls takes place primarily through linguistic channels and that this development is a fairly consistent one; in boys, however, the non-verbal skills clearly play a prominent but less predictable part in their intellectual development. This conclusion has been corroborated by the findings of a study of Oxfordshire schoolchildren; girls were seen to be more consistent in their intellectual development – their test performances at five years actually predicting scores on certain 11-plus tests.

Even more impressive perhaps are the results of the American longitudinal studies (e.g. Cameron, Livson and Bayley, 1967) since they cover a greater age-span. Girls once again were seen to focus on the vocal-verbal modality as early as five and a half months of age, and their infant babbles and vocalizations were good predictors of their subsequent intellectual development. The feminine tendency for accelerated development and increasing differentiation of linguistic features is further enhanced by the emphasis the mothers themselves, perhaps unwittingly, place on the vocal expressions of their infant daughters. Mothers more often talk to and imitate the babbles of their infant daughters than their sons (Moss, 1967). In fact the focus on the linguistic channels – pre-linguistic but vocal in infants – is so pronounced that even at a few months of age vocalizations are a good measure of attention in female infants. Similar vocalizations in boys are more indicative of a restless or active state (Kagan, 1969). It is interesting to find this essentially feminine propensity manifest in other primate species too, particularly where the female indicates her affective state by characteristic vocalizations.

One factor, however, qualifies the female supremacy in verbal skills. Many of the abilities we have discussed hitherto may be seen as referring to the *executive* aspects of language – reading, writing, spelling, and so on. In terms of verbal *reasoning*, on the other hand, the evidence is that girls no longer have the advantage. If we consider the normative scores for girls and boys at two ages on the Differential Aptitude Test (DAT), a test of different abilities by Bennett, Seashore and Wesman (1959), this distinction becomes clear:

Age	Sex	Verbal reasoning Mean	Language usage I: spelling Mean	Language usage II: sentences Mean
13	Boys	15·8	25·9	20·2
	Girls	14·6	37·9	28·6
17	Boys	29·3	59·1	40·9
	Girls	25·2	72·1	45·8

The girls at both ages score higher than the boys on measures of language usage but not on tests of verbal reasoning. Indeed, the boys' superiority in terms of verbal reasoning increases with age. Despite the girls' verbal fluency and precocity, their comprehension and reasoning in this area appear to be less adequate than the boys'. Tyler summarizes the relevant evidence thus:

Most of the available evidence seems to indicate . . . that it is in verbal *fluency* (what Thurstone has called W), rather than in the grasp of verbal meanings (V), that females are superior (1965).

Practical abilities

As a result, in part, of their superior visuo-spatial abilities, boys and men are also more proficient at mechanical tasks. This ability concerns not merely the execution of tasks like the servicing of motors, the installation of heating systems or the construction of some edifice, but also the *comprehension* of mechanical relationships, which is a more conceptual exercise. In an extensive application of the Mechanical Comprehension Test which requires the interpretation of mechanical relationships pictorially represented, men scored higher than women on every one of the sixty problems (Tyler, 1965). At a more individual level, only 5 per cent of the women and girls exceed the male average, indicating that the degree of overlap between males and females in this respect is relatively small.

In numerical and mathematical abilities too, boys and men fare better. This ability may not necessarily be evident at an early age, since it is chiefly 'mechanical' arithmetic with which children concern themselves. In such computational exercises girls do reasonably well. It is in the more complex mathematical reasoning and in the solution of problems involving the manipulation of abstract numerical entities, such as negative numbers, that boys excel.

In any tasks requiring manual dexterity, however, girls have the advantage. They are particularly skilful and deft with their hands, which may be one reason that women often are, and enjoy being, seamstresses and needlewomen. Even in industry those tasks calling for swift and dexterous assembly of small components are performed better by women. A technical film made by one of our leading electronic firms showed the miniaturized circuitry for components being assembled entirely by women. This dexterity results in women generally being extremely competent typists too, and it is a competence that men find difficult to match. Occasionally, of course, a man will show exceptional facility in such performances, like the man who won a recent Secretary-of-the-Year award; this award, however, was made on the basis of several abilities, only one of which was typing. In general, men require a good deal more training and experience than do women to perform on a par with them in clerical tasks (Garai and Scheinfeld, 1968).

Another characteristically feminine facility, which is not itself a practical ability but which may well aid in the execution of them, is that for rote memory. Women are able to hold in their memory store for short periods of time a number of unrelated and personally irrelevant facts, where men are only capable of comparable memory feats if the material is personally relevant or coherent. This particular aptitude would further enhance the female's value in secretarial and executive capacities. It seems to be more a sex-dependent facility than a skill readily cultivated in certain occupations.

There was general agreement among the boys and girls we talked to that many girls learn by memorizing material whether they understand it or not, whereas boys are more likely to try to master the underlying principles (Douglas, Ross and Simpson, 1968).

Exploration

The males of most mammalian species are the more exploratory members, and man is no exception. Although the great feats of territorial exploration are open to very few, exploration of a much more mundane kind goes on all around us. Some of the most fascinating exploratory pursuits are those undertaken by young children in learning about their environment. This exploratory activity, initiated by curiosity, is particularly evident when confronted with something new – a new toy, an unexpected sound or sight.

Studies of such exploratory behaviour of about 120 two- to five-year-old children revealed many differences between the boys and the girls (Hutt, 1970 a, b). Despite the fact that girls have been found to be less curious than boys (Smock and Holt, 1962; Mendel, 1965), we found no difference in the amount of curiosity and interest shown by boys and girls when presented with a completely new toy. There were, however, some salient and significant behavioural differences. For instance, there were some children who appeared to show no curiosity or interest in the toy (non-explorers) and these were more often girls than boys. Of the children who investigated and explored the toy (non-creative explorers), some went on to use it in many imaginative ways in their play (creative explorers), and most of these were boys. These results are summarized in Figure 27.

All children need to explore and investigate things around them in order to learn about the properties and functions of common objects such as light-switches and taps. (It is activity of this kind that often harasses mothers who are attempting to complete some routine task.) Thus, to find children who are unexploratory in the face of novelty is surprising. The fact that more girls than boys failed to explore could be explained in terms of the greater linguistic maturity of the former. Once children, and girls in particular, become verbally proficient, perhaps they are less interested in active and manipulatory exploration. On the other hand, there were certain behavioural clues picked up during these observations which suggested to us that these non-exploratory girls were nervous or anxious, but this interpretation required further investigation.

Again, the preponderance of boys amongst the 'creative explorers' could not be explained very easily. It could not be due to the fact that the toy appealed more to the boys than to the girls, since both were equally interested in it. It did however raise the possibility that here, in play, we were witnessing the origins of creative talent. In other words, was it possible that those children who were imaginative and inventive in their play were more likely subsequently to show creative and divergent thinking?

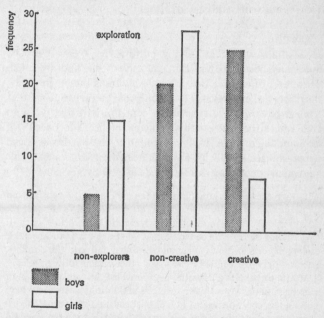

Figure 27 Number of girls and boys who showed different types of exploratory activity (see text)

A follow-up study made it possible for us to suggest some answers to these questions. This study was carried out on a proportion of the earlier sample. These children are now at primary school and aged between seven and ten years (Hutt and Bhavnani, 1972). Briefly, the results showed that the reasons for the lack of exploration were different for boys and for girls: in the case of the boys it was simply because they were not curious, but were rather apathetic and inactive individuals; the girls, on the other hand, were impeded by what we might call personality difficulties – on personality tests as well as parents' and teachers' ratings they turned out to be tense, anxious and timid individuals. The boys and girls who were 'creative explorers', however, were not very different in terms of personality features or social adjustment, but they did differ greatly in their performance on tests of creativity. This finding will be discussed further in the following section.

Creativity

It is noteworthy that in any culture the creative artists, musicians, scientists and thinkers have been, and are, men. There are, of course, exceptions in all areas but, regrettably, they remain exceptions. It is only as literary figures that women have made a substantial contribution, that is, in an area where they have a singular advantage. The paucity of feminine talent is generally attributed to the particular social circumstances in which women find themselves. A persuasive statement concerning this was made in 1947 by Terman:

Although the women equal or excel the men in school achievement from the first grade through college, after school days are over the great majority cease to compete with men in the world's work. If they do not marry at once they accept whatever kind of respectable employment is at hand. After marriage they fall into the domestic role and only in exceptional cases seek other outlets for their talents. The woman who is a potential poet, novelist, lawyer, physician or scientist usually gives up any professional ambition she may have had and devotes herself to home, husband and children. The exclusive devotion of women to domestic pursuits robs the arts and sciences of a large fraction of the genius that might otherwise be dedicated to them. My data strongly suggests that this loss must be debited to motivational causes and to limitations of opportunity rather than to lack of ability.

But Terman missed the point: about ability there has been little dispute. It is precisely in those para-intellectual qualities that determine creativity that men and women appear to differ – in orientation or cognitive style, in motivation or drive, in ambition.

Moreover, the 'social limitation' hypothesis, so ardently supported by the Women's Liberation Movement, does not stand up to close scrutiny. As Tyler has pointed out in her book, even in those areas which are traditionally the domain of women – cookery, needlework, hairdressing – the innovators, the leaders, the theoreticians so to speak, are most frequently men. Maccoby (1966) cites a most informative study: a sample of Radcliffe College academics was compared with a male sample of equal status, qualification and experience. Irrespective of discipline, and most important, of domestic commitment, the women published 'substantially less' than the men. Evidence of this kind suggests that men more often have a capacity for divergent and imaginative thinking, as well as a greater drive to bring their ideas to fruition. This latter characteristic will be given greater consideration in the next chapter.

In view of the positive association between creative productivity and performance on tests of creativity, it is particularly curious that psychologists interested in the processes of divergent thinking and in the development of creative talent have not observed or commented upon sex differences in this respect. Sex differences may not be noted for any one of three reasons: (a) they may not be looked for; (b) they may be found but not considered important by the investigator; (c) only one sex may be examined. Two fairly exhaustive reviews in recent years have indeed chastised psychologists for too often being culpable in this manner (Carlson and Carlson, 1960; Garai and Scheinfeld, 1968).

In order to obtain some normative data from primary school children (none being available for British children) against which to evaluate the results of our follow-up study, we examined the performance of sixty boys and sixty girls on a test of creativity (Bhavnani and Hutt, 1972). The test used was the widely applied test devised by Wallach and Kogan (1965). It consists of items such as 'How many uses can you think of for a tyre?', or 'What does this pattern make you think of?'

Tests of this type principally measure two aspects of thinking – Fluency and Originality. Fluency refers to the total number of responses given and Originality to the number of *unique* responses. To a certain extent the latter is dependent upon the former, since an individual produces the fairly conventional, stereotyped responses first and then goes on to give the more unusual, idiosyncratic ones. Since the verbal fluency of girls is well documented, and since the responses to these tests are

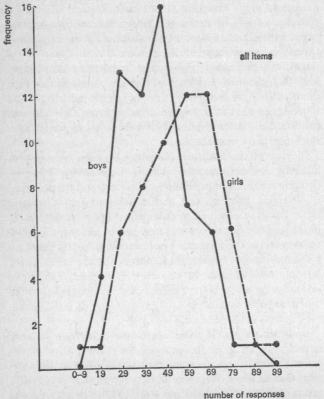

Figure 28 The distributions of the Fluency scores of sixty boys and sixty girls on the Wallach–Kogan test of creativity
(from Bhavnani and Hutt, 1972)

verbal, we expected to find that girls scored higher on this measure than boys – and they did (Figure 28). Although there is a good deal of overlap (and this would be expected), the distributions of scores for the boys and girls are significantly different. If the sexes do not differ in cognitive style – that is, in the manner in which they approach problems or the manner in which they construe aspects of their environment – then we would expect to find that girls score higher on Originality too, since they already have some advantage in Fluency. The results showed that in fact there were no differences. This finding indicates that, at this age, despite their greater fluency, girls are not necessarily more original than boys. At a later age, when boys have acquired greater verbal proficiency, one might expect boys to score higher than girls on the Originality measure.

In fact, the results of a recent and extensive study of young adults bears out this prediction (Shouksmith, 1970). Shouksmith was concerned with the interrelationships between intelligence, cognitive style and creativity, and used tests which tapped many aspects of cognitive style and expression. His conclusions from the results were as follows:

... males and females do not think alike. Factorially the female group is more complex than the male.... For females a much greater range of behaviour patterns appear to be mutually exclusive categories ... for example, we see that 'creative associating' is opposed to 'deductive reasoning' in women, where it is not so clearly opposed in men ... true creativity depends on an ability to switch from the one to the other of these as and when necessary. On this argument, one would expect to find fewer women among the ranks of truly inventive geniuses or scientific discoverers.

However, the generalization that males are more divergent in their thinking than females may be a little unfair to the latter. After all, the material with which the subject is confronted in these tests is largely of a non-personal, even neutral, nature. What Little (1968) has found is that where objects, things and abstract concepts are concerned, boys show greater cognitive complexity, but where personalities and values are concerned, girls show greater complexity. To put it another way, boys are *object-oriented* and have better differentiated concepts with respect to impersonal matters; girls, being *person-oriented*, differentiate more subtly along social and emotional dimensions. These characteristic differences in orientation will be taken up in more detail in the next chapter.

To return now to the results of the 'creative explorers' in our follow-up study, we found that the boys and girls did not differ greatly from each other in terms of their personality characteristics or social adjustment: independence and assertiveness seemed to characterize both sexes. But teachers often complained of boys in this group being 'disruptive influences in the class-room'; the girls apparently were not similarly culpable. This is probably due to the fact that assertive and adventurous boys are less tractable than assertive girls and that the teachers who had to cope with them were women.

In terms of their creativity scores, however, they differed considerably: the boys scored much higher than the girls. Furthermore, the correlation between the amount of imaginative or inventive play in early childhood and creativity scores in late childhood was significant for boys but not for girls. These findings seem to indicate two things: first, that in general, boys have a more divergent cognitive style where objects, concepts and ideas are concerned, and secondly that this style is expressed and can be discerned in the play of the pre-school child.

Educational implications of early sex differences

The differences between the sexes discussed in this and the preceding chapter have certain implications for education, particularly where the recognition of individual differences is concerned. One of these is that, due to their earlier maturation, the lack of nursery-school education is likely to be a more severe deprivation for girls than for boys. Between the ages of three and five years the girls are passing through a proportionately greater part of their formative period. The principles of numbers, for example, are acquired early in life and to a large extent non-linguistically. Is it possible that earlier and more systematic exposure of girls to the materials whereby numerical relationships may be explored may improve their subsequent skill in this respect?

Due both to their earlier maturation and their linguistic proficiency, girls secure more grammar-school places than boys. Hitherto, this fact has not proved a problem since in general the sexes are not in competition for such places. In those cases where they are, however, the boys may be at a grave disadvantage. Such competition would be particularly unfortunate, since in adolescence boys catch the girls up and even surpass them in certain skills. Moreover, the predictive value of an examination like the 11-plus would be different for boys and for girls.

Co-educational schools are desirable, if only for social reasons. Educationally, they may have problems, particularly with the younger classes where the sex-disparity is likely to be greatest. But it would be interesting to see if such schools would succeed in modifying some of the sex-patterns currently manifest and described by Dale (1970). Would, for instance, the number of girls leaving school prematurely be reduced? Would girls and boys take comparable subject loads? Would more girls take Mathematics, Physics and Chemistry, and more boys take Biology? And would the flagging performance of the girls in their later school years (Douglas, Ross and Simpson, 1968) be redressed?

Dale also points out that comparisons between the examination performances of boys and girls are apt to be misleading for the simple reason that at O-level, A-level and university, the sample of girls is more highly selected than the sample of boys. Comparisons would therefore tend to underestimate the performance of the boys, or apparently equalize where no parity exists. For instance, similar rates of Grade A passes by boys and girls in the A-level examination are interpreted by Dale quite correctly as indicating 'that the male sex had ... more "high flyers" than their share'.

Since remedial classes have to cater more frequently for boys than for girls, it seems that educational institutions are called upon to take practical note of the principle of greater variability in the male.

8 Aggression, Ambition and Affiliation

The evolutionary perspective

This chapter is concerned with the social behaviours, interests, attitudes and predispositions that are characteristic of the two sexes. Since many of these differences are not confined to the human species and are the consequence of distinctive reproductive roles, it may be more instructive to consider them in evolutionary perspective.

The species *homo sapiens*, on the most recent estimate, is only thirty-five million years old. In evolutionary terms, this is a very young age indeed. Man evolved from apes ancestral to the chimpanzee and gorilla. His acquisition of an erect posture and bipedalism were perhaps the most significant factors in his evolution. Bipedalism freed the upper limbs which then could be developed for manipulation, tool-using and hunting. Concurrently there was greater cephalization and the development of an enlarged cranium and brain, which in turn necessitated the development of a larger pelvis in the female. Due to the limitation of pelvic size, however, some development of the brain had to be deferred until after birth, and it is notable that man is the only species in which such a considerable amount of cerebral development takes place postnatally – up to the end of the second decade in fact. As a consequence of this immaturity, the period of infant dependency was protracted and more parental care and nursing were required. The greater dependence of the infant, together with the more flexible and prehensile upper limbs, which were thereby less adequate for grasping, meant that the young could no longer be easily transported and that the females and young had to adopt a less mobile mode of life. This meant a greater distinction between the roles of males and females:

males traversed wide spaces hunting in packs or groups; females remained within their territory or 'home', nurturing the young. It is not surprising, then, that distinctive structural and complementary functional features were evolved in males and females.

Good vision and sense of direction were of advantage to the hunter in locating his prey; so also were agility and strength, particularly of the upper arms – hence the greater development of bone and muscle in general and the biceps and deltoid muscles in particular in the male. Moreover, since hunting was a group activity, both the propensity for aggression – in predation and in order to maintain some position in a hierarchy – as well as the ability to cooperate and to derive pleasure from being in the company of other males would be a distinct advantage for the male. Conversely, the skills of nurture and repair would be advantageous to the female. For the effective performance of such skills, increasing reliance would be placed on the means of communication and there would be concern with the transmission of social mores and conventions. In this manner the differentiation of structures and abilities aided survival and was in turn promoted by the particular selective pressures which operated differentially on the male and on the female.

It is important to note that species survival refers not to the individual but to his genes. In other words, in evolutionary terms, the physical fitness or success of a particular individual is irrelevant if he leaves no progeny since his contribution to the gene pool, the genetic reservoir of the breeding group, is nil. Thus, sickle cell anaemia is lethal for the individual who possesses the gene in its homozygous condition; it is nevertheless advantageous for the population of certain territories to maintain this gene in its gene pool since it confers immunity to malaria when expressed in its heterozygous condition.

The evolutionary heritage of modern man then probably predisposed the males to be more aggressive, more exploratory, more vigorous and more group-oriented, and the females to be relatively more passive and dependent, more nurturant, more verbal, more concerned with morals and social conventions and less adventurous. We have already seen that there is considerable evidence for differences in sensory and executive skills which enable these predispositions to be manifest. In the rest of this chapter attention will be focused on particular aspects of these predispositions.

Aggression

In the majority of species, and certainly mammalian ones, the male is more aggressive than the female (Collias, 1944). The human species is no exception. From a very young age, boys are more aggressive than girls and until old age men are more aggressive than women. In all societies the delinquent and criminal populations are predominantly male.

The greater proneness of the male for manifesting aggressive behaviour is often interpreted in terms of learning, training and cultural influences. This environmentalist argument usually goes something like this: from a very early age, parents tolerate the expression of aggression in boys, whereas it is firmly discouraged in girls; as children grow older they emulate and identify with adults of their own sex, and since men manifest more aggression, boys see aggression as an appropriate, and even desirable, masculine trait. No one ever seems to have questioned why this should be so. Why should parents permit greater aggressiveness in their sons than in their daughters? Why should the sex-stereotype be of an aggressive male and a passive and docile female?

Social conventions usually have some rational basis, particularly if they prevail in a number of societies, many of them differing radically in other cultural mores. Moreover, the attitudes of a particular society change with time and this applies especially to patterns of child-rearing, which have altered substantially in the last forty years. Nevertheless, a number of studies (nearly fifty in number) carried out in the United States over a period of thirty years – from 1933 to 1965 – quite unambiguously demonstrated that boys and men were more aggressive and hostile than girls and women (Oetzel, 1966; Feshbach, 1970). The only exceptions related to expressions of verbal aggression, which women tended to manifest more than men. More recent studies of pre-school children in this country too have demonstrated similar sex differences (Clark, Wyon and Richards, 1969; Brindley *et al.*, 1972; Hutt, 1972 a, b, c).

Any scientist interested in developmental processes, when confronted with such a consistent sex-dependent behavioural phenomenon which prevails despite changes in time and space, and which is shared by other species of some phylogenetic affinity, is constrained to examine the biological origins of such a phenomenon. For biological origins there must be. In carrying out such an examination there is no repudiation of environmental or social factors. Neither is there an assumption of an antithesis between biological and social processes. Can a gene express itself other than in some environmental condition? Do social and cultural factors operate on a *tabula rasa*? The manner of the interplay between biological and social factors should be our primary concern.

The biology of aggression

In all infra-human species aggression can be shown to confer some biological advantage on its exponent (Wynne-Edwards, 1962). Hamburg (1971) suggests that in primates, in the course of evolution, aggression may have conferred selective advantage in one or several of the following ways: 1. increasing the means of defence; 2. providing access to valued resources such as food, water and females in reproductive condition; 3. contributing to effective utilization of the habitat by distributing or spacing out animals in relation to available resources; 4. resolving serious disputes within the group; 5. providing a predictable, and hence stable, social environment; 6. providing leadership for the group, particularly in dangerous circumstances; 7. enabling differential reproduction – the more aggressive and more dominant males being more likely to pass on their genes because of their greater success in mating during peak receptivity.

Hamburg also observes that, for any species, there are some patterns of behaviour that are very easily learned, some that are less easy, and some that are exceedingly difficult; in general, it is those patterns of behaviour which have been of survival value that are easily learned. In fact, many such patterns are programmed as reflexes (e.g. the eye-blink), others come under more complex genetic and hormonal control.

The neuroendocrinological and experimental evidence shows that aggression is a function of three factors: 1. the early differentiation of the brain and neural structures according to a male pattern; 2. the level of circulating hormones, namely androgens; 3. particular environmental circumstances. We shall consider each of these factors in turn.

The male brain. Although aggression is primarily a socially directed behaviour it is extremely difficult to study it systematically in natural conditions since it is impossible to control all extraneous variables. For this reason many experimenters have confined their studies to analogous patterns of behaviour which can be reliably elicited in the laboratory and which can therefore be subjected to some degree of control and manipulation. These are isolation-induced aggression and shock-induced aggression.

When rodents are confined in isolation for a period of time they exhibit aggressive behaviour spontaneously or to minimal disturbance. Similarly, when rats are given a moderate electric shock, they show aggressive behaviour such as biting, threat, bristling. Although the justification for using these patterns of behaviour in experimental work is their similarity to normal aggressive behaviours, extrapolations from these results should be made with circumspection.

Males exhibit aggression under both these conditions far more frequently than females (see Figure 29). Not only is the frequency of fighting greater but the males also maintain the fighting stance for longer (Conner *et al.*, 1969). Ovariectomy of the adult female has no effect on the amount of fighting she displays, but castration of the adult male does depress the level of aggression slightly. Castration of the young male, however, considerably reduces the amount of aggression. Since in the rat sexual differentiation of the brain takes place soon after birth, the younger the rats are when castrated the less 'male' their

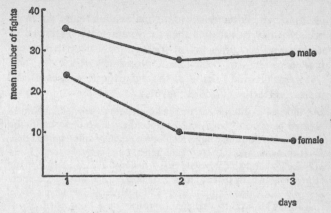

Figure 29 Mean number of fighting responses in pairs of male and female rats as a function of testing days
(from Conner *et al.*, 1969)

brains will be. Accordingly, if rats are castrated at weaning (about three weeks of age) their level of aggression in adulthood is considerably lower than that of intact males, but that of males castrated at birth is lower still and indistinguishable from the female level of aggression (see Figure 30). Conversely, if females are exposed to androgens in infancy, and their brains thereby masculinized, they show levels of fighting and aggression as adults comparable with those of normal males.

In monkeys, too, we saw earlier that females virilized by androgens before birth show more threat, attack, chasing and rough-and-tumble play than normal females. Males castrated at birth show no appreciable decrement in these behaviours, since at birth differentiation of the brain has already taken place. Similarly, we saw that human females exposed prior to birth to excessive androgenic influences were more 'tomboyish', physically vigorous and assertive than normal females.

It is conceivable of course that appreciable dosages of any steroid hormone, and particularly the androgens, may increase activity or vigour in the female organism as well, but the propensity for exhibiting aggressive behaviour as such seems to be a characteristic of the male rather than the female brain. It may be recalled that the infant monkeys raised in isolation with only a model for company nevertheless exhibited patterns of behaviour appropriate to their sex, and this was particularly true of the agonistic responses of the males. As Harlow (1965) comments:

It is illogical to interpret these sex differences as learned, culturally ordered patterns of behaviour because there is no opportunity for acquiring a cultural heritage, let alone a sexually differentiated one, from an inanimate cloth surrogate. When I first saw these data, I was very excited and told my wife that I believed that we had demonstrated biologically determined sex differences in infants' behaviour. She was not impressed and said 'Child psychologists have known that for at least thirty years, and mothers have known it for centuries.'

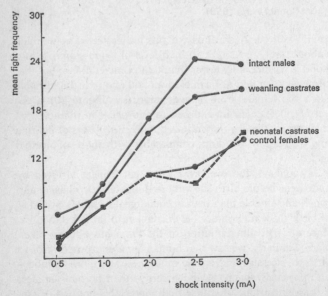

Figure 30 Mean fighting frequency in adulthood for intact, weanling age and neonatally castrated male rats and intact female rats, as a function of shock intensity (from Conner *et al.*, 1969)

Circulating hormones. Studies of this factor primarily concern adult animals, since the levels of circulating sex hormones in prepubertal animals and humans are very low. It is a general principle that adults will react more readily to hormones of their own sex than to those of the opposite sex (Conner *et al.*, 1969). Thus, while administration of testosterone will slightly increase the level of aggression in an adult male, it will have no effect whatsoever upon the female (Beeman, 1947; Tollman and King, 1956). In fact, in many cases testosterone *inhibits* aggression in the female and causes hyperfeminization (Neumann, Steinbeck and Hahn, 1970). Similarly, if a male rat castrated at birth is subsequently treated with androgens no effect is observed (Conner and Levine, 1969). The weanling castrates, on the other hand, do respond to testosterone. These findings show that level of androgens *per se* is ineffectual with respect to aggression unless masculine differentiation of the brain has already taken place.

The female hormone oestrogen has an inhibitory effect on aggression in males (Suchowsky, Pegrassi and Bonsignori, 1969) but its depletion has little effect on females.

More recently, evidence showing a direct relationship between levels of plasma testosterone and amount of aggression has become available. Rose and his colleagues (1971) have shown that male monkeys displaying more aggressive behaviour, eliciting more submissive behaviour from their subordinates, and occupying high positions in the dominance hierarchy also have higher levels of plasma testosterone than their less aggressive colleagues. Although which is cause and which effect is a matter of dispute, the evidence from humans, implicating endocrine dysfunction in some affective disturbances, suggests that the behavioural differences may, in some cases, be contingent upon hormonal factors. Even more dramatically, Persky, Smith and Basu (1971) have found a direct relationship between rate of production of testosterone and measures of aggression and hostility amongst normal adult males (see Figure 31). The measures of hostility and aggression were obtained from responses to tests which were adequately validated against overt expressions of these moods.

Interestingly, this relationship did not hold for older men, i.e. those over thirty years! This dependence of affective states upon endocrine function very probably accounts for some of the turbulence of the adolescent period: both boys and girls have to adapt, fairly suddenly, to high levels of circulating sex hormones. Whereas with oestrogens the situation may only be depressive, with androgens it is likely to be explosive!

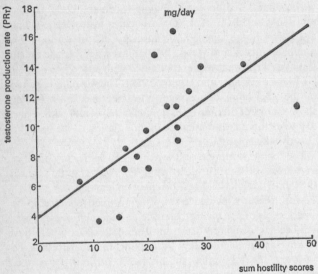

Figure 31 The relationship between the rate of production of testosterone and hostility scores in eighteen men between seventeen and twenty-eight years of age (from Persky, Smith and Basu, 1971)

Environmental factors. Irrespective of its hormonal level, a dominant monkey frequently shows more threat and attack than the sub-dominant animals. The dominance is usually a result of the outcomes of previous agonistic encounters. Again, the readiness with which an animal displays aggression depends on a variety of early experiences – whether it has been reared in isolation, whether it has experienced much fighting, whether it has been handled, and so on.

Bandura and his colleagues (1961) found that both boys and girls would imitate the aggressive behaviour of a model adult whom they had observed on a film. Nevertheless, whereas girls were equally ready to imitate the behaviour of a man as of a woman, boys were more reluctant to imitate the aggressive actions of a woman.

Increasing the number of children in a playroom increased the amount of aggression in normal children only slightly (Hutt and Vaizey, 1966); when the playroom was partitioned, however, thereby permitting territorial behaviour, the increase in aggression was considerably greater (Hutt and Hutt, 1970). Our studies of the social behaviour of pre-school children also illustrate a noteworthy interaction between innate predisposition and environmental opportunity. As Figure 32 shows, boys

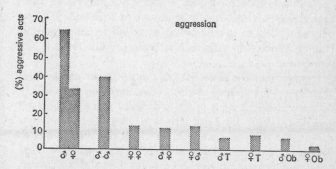

Figure 32 Aggressive behaviour manifested by boys and girls. The first pair of histograms shows the proportion of all aggressive acts committed by boys and girls respectively; subsequent histograms show to whom these acts were directed; boys to boys, girls to girls, boys to girls, girls to boys, boys to teachers, girls to teachers, boys to objects (toys, furniture etc.), and girls to objects (from Brindley et al., 1972)

are twice as aggressive as girls (aggression here including verbal aggression), but even more interesting is the fact that it is predominantly boys towards whom this aggression is directed. Boys also retaliate more and hence prolong such encounters, whereas the girls usually submit or else employ more devious strategies to secure their objectives. This contrast is nicely illustrated by the following instances:

Keith was pushing a wheel-barrow in which Colin was sitting. Robert approached and wanted to climb in too. Both Keith and Colin refused. The teacher intervened and said wouldn't it show how strong Keith was if he could push *both* boys. Reluctantly, Robert was allowed to climb in but all the while Keith pushed, Colin continued to jab kicks at Robert. The encounter was terminated when Robert asked to be set down.

Susan was filling jars and bottles at the water tank. When Stephen approached she said, 'No, go away, I'm playing here'. She was heard by a teacher who asked that Stephen be allowed to play too. Susan immediately gave Stephen the least attractive cup and partly broken 'squirter', reserving all the other vessels for herself. The teacher, satisfied with the apparent accession to her request, moved away, and Susan had conceded the minimum.

Girls differentiate much less amongst the objects of their aggression: they are equally aggressive to boys and girls and only a little less so to the teacher. Although verbal aggression is more frequent in girls than in boys, the difference is not significant.

The fact that the male not only more frequently *initiates* aggressive behaviours but also *elicits* them has been nicely demonstrated in a study of ten and eleven year olds (Shortell and Biller, 1970). Boys and girls were allegedly engaged in a competitive reaction-time task, in which the subject was to deliver a noise to a mock opponent if the latter was slower, and conversely the subject received a noise if he/she was slower. The experimenter in fact controlled both the opponent's speed of response and the level of sound-punishment administered to the subject. The various intensities of the noises had previously been rated by the subject and all 'punishments' administered to him were below the level of 'quite unpleasant'. A salutory sex difference emerged in the results: boys chose higher noise levels (usually rated unpleasant) when meting out punishment than did girls. When subjects thought their opponents were boys they administered harsher punishment (higher noise levels) than if they thought they were girls. An earlier study had shown that this peculiar ability of males not only to be 'vindictive' but also to elicit 'vindictiveness' was true of adults as well (Taylor and Epstein, 1967). When a similar task was carried out with undergraduates and with shock as punishment, males were found to be much more aggressive than the females. Once again male 'opponents' were treated more harshly than females, and increasingly so.

Ambition and drive

Closely related to aggression are these two characteristics of ambition and drive. There is often semantic confusion about the term aggression and it may seem irresponsible to add to this confusion by considering other, apparently tenuously, related conditions. But there are good reasons for doing so. First, aggression, ambition and drive all make reference to the *vigour* of behaviour; situational factors may indeed determine the particular expression but all three conditions are associated with a high degree of motivation. Secondly, there is a conceptual relationship; all concern competition – the achievement of a goal invariably at the expense of other individuals. In fact, we may more appropriately regard ambition as 'channelled drive'. It seems legitimate, therefore, to consider these as related aspects of man's behaviour, to inquire why the male of the species has the prerogative of such characteristics, and to suggest why they may serve an adaptive function, even in modern man.

From the clinical evidence Money (1965) concludes that 'androgen is the libido hormone for both men and women'. In women the source of the androgen is the adrenal gland and women who are deprived of their adrenal androgens – as in the treatment of breast cancer – suffer a great or complete loss of libido. Oestrogen, on the other hand, is what Money calls 'a functionally castrating agent'. It depresses libido and potency in men.

Indeed, it is not implausible to regard androgens as the *fons et origo* of all drive, sexual or otherwise. Here again the clinical evidence relating to a variety of conditions such as the adreno-genital syndrome, the testicular feminization syndrome,

Addison's disease, adrenalectomy, or hormonal treatment of trans-sexuals, strongly supports the relationship between androgens and drive.

A society needs to perpetuate itself by ensuring an adequate number of surviving progeny. This is ultimately dependent on the assiduous efforts of the male in courting and mating, efforts which are subserved by sexual libido. Similarly, non-sexual drive promotes achievement and success by enabling persistent effort in competitive situations. As Wynne-Edwards (1962) observes of animal societies in general:

Admission to the social group and advancement in social status within it appear to constitute one side of the dual prize to be sought in conventional competition: the other side, never perhaps wholly separable from it, takes the form of concrete possessions. In either event, the reward that comes from success is a matter of rights and privileges. Privilege is an exceedingly desirable prize, since without it the individual can be excluded from food, from reproduction, and from the habitat itself . . . .

In man, the privileges and rewards are often more intangible but nonetheless procurable by similar means. Aggression ostensibly may seem undesirable, but its elimination may have other untoward effects, such as the reduction of drive, ambition and hence achievement. It may be argued that all these features are dispensable, that what we require are non-competitive, non-acquisitive societies. How such societies operate and survive, whether indeed they are viable at all, are matters about which we know very little. What we do know is that those who have made the greatest impact on society – the artists and scientists, innovators, social reformers, statesmen – have done so by pursuing their objectives with determination and single-mindedness.

One way in which this achievement and single-mindedness may come about is by the neurohumoral control of attention. The administration of testosterone, for instance, has been shown to improve focusing of attention and to enhance the persistence with which an activity is continued once it has been initiated (Andrew and Rogers, 1972; Archer, 1971). Testosterone also alleviates fatigue (Klaiber et al., 1971) and facilitates sustained attention and performance on a repetitive task (Broverman *et al.*, 1968; Vogel *et al.*, 1971). Hamburg has implied too that the greater predisposition of the male for aggression may be mediated by attentional processes (1971).

But how would such effects come about? Clearly by the action of steroid hormones, and androgens in particular, upon the central nervous system. Welch (1967) suggests that the steroids which increase aggression do so primarily by enhancing the excitability of neurochemical receptors. He states:

... we now have very good reason to believe that the predominant neurotransmitter substances in subcortical activating systems are catecholamines, primarily norepinephrine. Of particular interest are reports that the pharmacologic enhancement of the release of brain amines dramatically increases the level of excitation, general arousal, and aggressiveness in a variety of animals, including mice, rats, rabbits, dogs and monkeys.

Androgens are known to have particularly striking effects on brain amines and a facilitatory action upon central nervous system excitability. Administration of androgen in early life results in increased concentrations of at least one neurotransmitter, serotonin (Ladosky and Gaziri, 1969), as well as in increased RNA synthesis in the brain (Shimada and Gorbman, 1970). As Bronson and Desjardins (1971) suggest:

Early androgenization results in an alteration in the rate of synthesis of specific enzyme systems that will later function in the adult by becoming more (or less?) active, given the presence of circulating androgens.

Thus we may have here a common neurochemical basis for aggression, drive and attention.

Feminine interests and values

In sharp contrast to these predispositions of the male are the altruism, the regard for intimacy and personal relationships, and the protective nurturance of the female. We have already seen in the previous chapter that in relation to persons, the cognitive complexity of the female is greater than that of the male. Similarly, even in scientific pursuits, women have a higher regard for social values and interpersonal needs than for more abstract matters of theory or political ideology. As long ago as 1931, Allport and Vernon employed the six 'values' of the German philosopher Spranger in their investigations of the attitudes and interests of different groups of people – socioeconomic groups, ethnic groups, occupational groups and so on. The six values are defined as follows:

Theoretical: interest in the pursuit of truth by intellectual means.
Economic: interest in useful, practical things.
Aesthetic: interest in beauty and art.
Social: interest in helping people.
Political: interest in power or influence over people.
Religious: interest in mystical experience.

Allport, Vernon and Lindzey (1951) found that men and women scored very differently on these six scales (see Figure 33): women had far greater aesthetic, social and religious interests, whereas men were more politically and theoretically inclined. These differences are borne out, both by other empirical evidence (see Oetzel, 1966) and in practice. Women are more concerned than men with moral issues; they protest more vehemently where they perceive injustice; they are more concerned with inculcating social mores and codes of conduct; they attend church more regularly. Men are more frequently the politicians, the theoreticians, the ideologists.

Girls consistently achieve better school grades than do boys, even in those subjects at which boys conventionally perform better. Their subsequent achievement, however, is considerably poorer than might have been expected. Although the superior school performance of the girls may, in part, be attributable to their advanced maturation and greater docility, their lack of subsequent achievement seems less explicable. Although many women devote at least some of their professional years to bringing up a family, the number of women in employment has nevertheless increased in the last two decades. This increase, however, is not reflected generally. For instance, in many scientific areas women continue to be severely

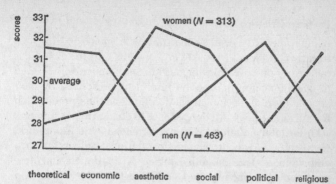

Figure 33 Composite psychographs of adult men and women on the Allport–Vernon study of values (from Tyler, 1965)

under-represented: over the period 1950–60 the proportion of women working in the natural sciences actually declined from 11 per cent to 9 per cent (Rossi, 1965).

In an attempt to find out why girls failed to achieve their earlier promise, particularly in science, Walberg (1969) studied the abilities, attitudes and personality traits of a large number of boys and girls studying physics at high school. On three of four cognitive tests (one of which was an I Q test) girls did better than the boys. These three tests tapped chiefly verbal factors; on the fourth test, which was concerned with numerical and spatial items, the boys were superior. In terms of their values on the Allport–Vernon test, once again girls displayed more interest in people and religious ideas while boys valued practicality, power and theoretical ideas. In summary:

Four distinguishing patterns of differences were identified; the girls were higher on all four: verbal aptitude (but not quantitative and spatial abilities), social values and interpersonal needs, cautiousness especially about science experiences, and aesthetic (rather than theoretical) valuations. These factors may lead to greater academic success in high school but appear to penalize women for later eminence in scientific careers.

Thus, the very psychological dispositions of women appear to militate against great achievements in competitive fields. But should this be an occasion for lament?

Person orientation

In interpreting the results of his study of language development in early childhood, Moore (1967) suggests that the girls focus quite early on developing linguistic skills because of their need to communicate, this need in turn being prescribed by their greater interest in personal relationships and their predilection for nurturant roles. All the evidence to date certainly supports such an interpretation. Within a psychoanalytic framework, Gutmann (1965) contrasts the 'maturational milieux' of men and women: the masculine milieu is an impersonal one, governed by principles and laws; the feminine milieu is a personal one of family and community, governed by feelings and shared goals. Gutmann surmises that different capacities would be adaptive to the psychological 'habitats' of men and women.

Taking Gutmann's formulations as her point of departure, Carlson (1971) carried out a number of imaginative studies which demonstrated many characteristic differences between the sexes in their conception of themselves and their environment. Males tended to represent themselves in individualistic or personal terms, i.e. not requiring a social object (e.g. 'ambitions', 'idealistic'), whereas females did so in interpersonal or social terms. Males represented others in objective, 'demographic' terms (e.g. 'Miss L. is a twenty-four-year-old divorcee employed as a stenographer'), females in more subjective, interpretative terms. Similar differences appeared too in the manner in which males and females construed their physical environment. Finally, males portrayed the future 'in terms of instrumental actions and external change', while females did so 'in terms of interpersonal events and inner change'; for example 'family' was mentioned by twenty out of twenty-eight females, but only nine out of twenty-seven males. The consistency of the differences in these diverse sets of constructs is impressive.

Even male and female academics conceive their professional identities differently: men are more concerned with academic prestige and institutional power, women with developing students, fostering scholarship and promoting institutional service (Bernard, 1964). These differences in construing their academic roles, may, in part, account for the 'disappointing' performance of the Radcliffe College Ph.Ds. mentioned in the last chapter. As Maccoby observed of those results:

... women who are as well off as men (or perhaps better off) with respect to alternative demands on their time are nevertheless less productive. It is difficult to attribute this fact to anything about the professional roles they currently occupy (1966).

While men are generally found to be autonomous and independent, women are more conforming and persuasible (Hovland and Janis, 1959; Douvan, 1960). These particular personality orientations appear to develop and stabilize during early adolescence (Carlson, 1965). Many studies, however, suggest that the origins of these are discernible as early as childhood (see Mischel, 1970).

Affiliation

Affiliation refers to the tendency of one individual to seek the proximity of another and to derive pleasure from doing so. In our studies of nursery-school children we found that this was a predominant tendency of the little girls – they spent by far the greatest proportion of time in social interaction of one kind or another, while the boys more frequently were engaged in some physical activity, e.g. wood-work, running and chasing, or playing with push/pull toys. The greater affiliative propensities of the girls were also evident in a behaviour we called 'Co-operation'. This consisted of those instances where two or more children joined each other, spontaneously or at the request of one of them, to engage in some mutual activity or exchange. Here are illustrative examples of spontaneous and requested cooperation:

Jeanette goes to the animal house and picks up a guinea pig. Fiona comes across and joins her and strokes the guinea pig. Both stroke the animal while Jeanette holds it. Fiona then gets the water-trough and holds it for the guinea pig to drink. Jeanette is still holding it.

Louise has difficulty fastening her shoe. She goes up to Barbara and requests help, holding out her foot. Barbara bends down, fastens the shoe while Louise also bends to watch her. Barbara straightens up and smiles at Louise who says 'Thank you' and runs off.

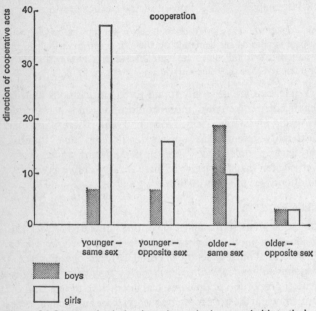

Figure 34 Cooperative behaviour shown by boys and girls to their peers : the first pair of histograms shows the proportion of all such acts which boys directed towards younger boys and girls towards younger girls ; the second pair shows those which boys directed to younger girls and girls towards younger boys, and so on (from Brindley *et al.*, 1972)

Girls exhibited this kind of behaviour much more frequently than boys (Figure 34) but additionally, girls directed their attention in this respect chiefly to *younger* children, and boys to older children than themselves. These differences in fact reflect the predominant tendency of the girls to perform a care-taking and protective role – aiding younger infants in carrying heavy objects, helping button pinafores or tie aprons etc. (see Figure 35) – and the equally predominant tendency of

Figure 35 A 'cooperative' act typical of girls: an older girl
buttoning the shoe of a younger girl (drawn by Jill Watson)

the boys to attach themselves to older boys and attempt to join in their activities (Figure 36). Such sex differences in children's spontaneous behaviour are customarily interpreted in terms of the learning and imitation of sex-appropriate behaviours, though, as we remarked earlier, such an interpretation still begs the question of why certain patterns of behaviour are judged to be more appropriate to one sex than the other. It is therefore instructive to note that similar differences have been found in rhesus monkeys, squirrel monkeys, baboons, langurs and chimpanzees (see Hutt, 1972 a, c).

A striking example of the contrast between the nurturant, protective attitude typical of the female, and the casual, indifferent attitude of the male – reactions which are evident as early as three or four years of age – is given by McGrew (1972) in his description of the nursery-school child's reaction to a newcomer:

Girls seemed to attend more to newcomers than boys, and several girls ... displayed a remarkable degree of maternalistic attentiveness ... soothing tones were accompanied by tactile comforting: holding hands, hugging, hand on child's back, arm around shoulders, patting, kissing. ... Boys could be friendly to newcomers, but most seemed to exhibit indifference ... The three male older siblings observed (Ivan, Norman, Homer) did not spend as much time with their newly-introduced siblings as did the female older siblings. Homer and Ivan virtually ignored them unless the younger sibling initiated interaction while Norman alternated between seeming 'protectiveness' and 'annoyance' at being followed about. One older sibling, Cora, completely dominated her younger brother Tommy's first day. They entered the nursery holding hands, and throughout the morning's first play period she steered him from activity to activity, monopolizing his attention.

Same-sex preferences

A notable feature that emerges from our own studies, as well as those of other workers, is the marked tendency for boys and girls to interact with their own sex. Apart from relatively brief or transient encounters with a member of the opposite sex the propensity for forming like-sex pairs or groups is evident throughout the pre-school period.

Figure 36 A 'cooperative' act typical of boys : two younger boys attempting to join a game played by older boys (drawn by Jill Watson)

Indeed, this seems to be an ubiquitous finding since it is evident in older children, adults and sub-human primates. Particularly interesting were the preferences observed in rhesus monkeys: young monkeys under seven months of age showed no consistent preference for peers of either sex; in childhood, so to speak, they showed an unambiguous preference for peers of the same sex, and as 'adolescents' for peers of the opposite sex, the preference for the opposite sex occurring earlier in females; with respect to adults, however, all monkeys under thirty-eight months of age preferred female adults to male and all monkeys over forty months preferred adults of their own sex (Suomi *et al.*, 1970).

The preferences of pre-school children too are manifest in characteristically different ways: when boys are gathered together it is generally as a group of three or more, and their attention tends to be focused on some activity or on objects (see Figure 37); girls, on the other hand, tend to assort in pairs and are most often concerned with intimate interaction *per se* (see Figure 38). The essentially feminine coffee-mornings, as well as the more ritualized Rotarian nights, Freemasonry and Forestry of the males are simply adult human extensions of natural proclivities which are already manifest in our ontogenetic kith and phylogenetic kin! It is interesting that much of the ritual that characterizes male groups in terms of dress and convention is characteristic too of the epidiectic displays of the males of other species.

What is particularly noteworthy is that many of the attitudes, interests and behaviours discussed in this chapter appear to be relatively independent of the type of society and culture in which the individuals are reared. Whiting (1963) studied six cultures as varied as India, Okinawa, the Philippines, Mexico, Kenya and New England and found essentially similar patterns of male and female behaviour. As John Whiting observes:

We have behavioral observations on boys and girls in six different societies up to the age of six, and in each of these societies girls behave in a way that we have called 'Domures'. A factor analysis of the behaviour shows three things: dominance, nurturance and

Figure 37 Typical group activities of nursery-school boys (drawn by Jill Watson)

Figure 38 Typical interaction between nursery-school girls
(drawn by Jill Watson)

responsibility, and this combination is essentially the definition of what a mother is to her children. She must be dominant, she nurtures and does the care taking, and she is responsible. We find that girls show these types of behavior in each of the six cultures which are located in six parts of the world entirely unrelated to another. Girls exhibit this at an earlier age and more than boys do. Conversely, in each of these six cultures, boys are characterized by more physical attack, more physical aggression, than are girls. This seems to me to indicate an underlying difference in the physiological wiring of the two sexes (1965).

Indeed, when we find sex differences which prevail as consistently over time, space, and species, as those discussed in this chapter, it seems highly improbable that they are entirely culturally ordained.

9 Men, Women and Society

In the preceding chapters we have examined how the process of sexual differentiation comes about and how the anatomical and physiological differences between the sexes are complemented by behavioural and psychological differences. An inventory of human sex differences *per se* would hardly be edifying – besides, such differences have been adequately documented in many recent reviews (Terman and Tyler, 1954; Tyler, 1965; Maccoby, 1966; Garai and Scheinfeld, 1968). It is far more instructive to inquire how such differences arise and what factors can modify or eradicate them, or indeed whether it is desirable to do so.

It must be emphasized once again that we have been describing and discussing males and females *in general*, not any particular man or woman, and the degree of overlap on any performance or function is appreciable. Nevertheless, the *patterning* of abilities is characteristically different in men and women. To recapitulate, we have seen that the male is physically stronger but less resilient, he is more independent, adventurous and aggressive, he is more ambitious and competitive, he has greater spatial, numerical and mechanical ability, he is more likely to construe the world in terms of objects, ideas and theories. The female at the outset possesses those sensory capacities which facilitate interpersonal communion; physically and psychologically she matures more rapidly, her verbal skills are precocious and proficient, she is more nurturant, affiliative, more consistent, and is likely to construe the world in personal, moral and aesthetic terms.

We have seen that for many of these characteristic features there are biological bases. For success, it has been provident to have the more adaptive behaviours under some measure of genetic control. These behaviours are adaptive in terms of the reproductive roles that males and females fulfil: the conformity and consistency of the female makes her a reliable and dependable source of nurture for the infant in its protracted dependency; for more effective communication and socialization a greater emphasis and reliance on linguistic skills and moral propensities has proved valuable; for the exploring and resource-hunting male in turn, a facility for dealing with spatial and conceptual relationships, for reasoning, for divergence in thought and action, has proved equally useful. Many of these features are not of contemporary origin, but have both a phylogenetic and ontogenetic history.

Overlying these biological bases are a multitude of social and cultural influences which operate from the moment of birth. We have seen, for example, that the mother imitates, and thereby reinforces, the babbling of her infant daughter more than that of her infant son. This fact very probably helps to emphasize even further the vocal and verbal proclivities of the female. And by the age of three years boys and girls begin to identify with the parent of the same sex. They attempt to imitate the actions of and to accept the interests and values of that parent. The evidence from families where the father has been absent for a prolonged period of time shows that the boys have less masculine interests; this finding certainly suggests that there are strong parental influences shaping and moulding the attitudes and orientations of the young. But such influences operate upon an already differentiated organism – an organism that already has a predisposition to sense and act in one way rather than another. Parents, society, or culture operate to modulate or amplify the predispositions already extant; it is doubtful whether they can fashion these completely anew; or whether it is desirable that they should. It is here that biology and social reform come into conflict.

Any resolution of this conflict demands that an implicit confusion be made explicit. That sex differences do exist is an incontrovertible *biological* fact. Whether such differences should result in differential treatment of males and females is a *social* decision. Equality does not mean similarity. Yet this is a confusion only too evident in the declamations of many feminists: 'There are no differences between men and women except for minor anatomical features'; 'anything you can do, I can do better'. Our society accords the same rights to education, to medical care and to social benefits to all its citizens, whatever their race, colour or creed, or is in principle committed to doing so. Similarly, there can be no justification whatsoever for discriminating between men and women in terms of these fundamental community rights. But these are rights that a society, by consensus, confers upon its members and they are not achieved by the repudiation of biological differences.

Thus, there can be no excuse for differential rates of pay for men and women doing the same job. Nor can there be any justification for debarring men or women from a particular trade or profession. To be sure, a female steeple-jack or coal-miner is rather unlikely but it should not be declared impossible at the outset. Acknowledging that the sexes differ in characteristic ways but that there is a fair degree of overlap too, the same considerations should apply to the selection of women *vis-à-vis* men as apply to the selection of men *vis-à-vis* one another. If, then, a man, or a woman, is selected for the job, one is at least prepared to be persuaded that it is on grounds of suitability for the job rather than on grounds of the sex of the applicant.

On the other hand, there are certain factual reasons why men and women cannot, at present, be considered equivalent employees. For instance, the fact that in some industries women are paid a lower wage is because they do different types of work and also work shorter hours than men – thirty-eight hours as opposed to forty-six hours by men (Davies, 1970). The turnover rate too is higher for women than for men. Women are debarred, by legislation, from working at night without special dispensation, and from working more than forty-eight hours a week. Women are proscribed by the Ministry of Labour from lifting weights in excess of sixty-five pounds; men are permitted to carry up to a hundred and fifty pounds. The productivity and working capacity of women in many industrial activities appears to be lower than that of men (Davies, 1970). These factors make it unlikely that, in industrial occupations at least, men and women are subjected to the same considerations.

However, other discriminative procedures prevail because of the legacy of social history. The prior exclusion of women from the stock market or their preclusion from undertaking hire-purchase contracts, seems to have little rational foundation. The persistence of such anachronisms in the latter part of the twentieth century, irrespective of the circumstances of the individuals, seems preposterous. The efforts of activist feminist groups to have this kind of injustice redressed are laudable, and should be encouraged.

We live, we are told, in a man's world. This is meant to imply that women have no choice in the matter of their occupation, that perforce they are relegated to menial and unrewarding duties and that, even when they break out of their chains of domesticity they are precluded, by men, from entering many professions of their choice. But, in the absence of independent evidence for discrimination against women, both the inference from, and the explanation of, the facts in terms of discrimination amounts to a tautology. In other words, evidence *other* than the poor representation of women in the professions, for instance, has to be adduced to explain their poor representation. In fact, the evidence shows that even when and where there is economic and social equality, as in the more egalitarian and emancipated societies of the Soviet Union or Communist China, the major policy decisions, whether in politics, the arts, the sciences or social services, are nonetheless made by men. The best documented evidence in this respect comes from studies of the kibbutzim (Bettelheim, 1969; Gerson, 1971), and merits some scrutiny.

In the kibbutz, both men and women are economically independent. Domestic chores are reduced to a minimum and women are expected to play a full and active part in all spheres of social and administrative life. But after the initial period of intense ideological commitment, it seems that the women have become more disillusioned with the *status quo* than have the men. They resent the almost complete delegation of the care of their offspring to the *metapelets* and play a surprisingly smaller part in planning, administration and management than might have been expected. The women now tend to marry younger despite the fact that they sacrifice the opportunity for vocational training by doing so. Gerson summarizes his several observations as follows:

Young women, rejoining the kibbutz after army service, wish to begin as early as possible to build their family nests. . . . Job involvement seems to be weaker among young women in the kibbutz than are family considerations; when job and family conflict, preference is given to the latter, as indicated by the trend to early marriage.

Thus, with all the achievements of the kibbutz, two basic problems of women remain: dissatisfaction in the sphere of work, and comparatively little participation in civic activities and the management of the society.

After two generations of repudiation of traditional sex roles, the kibbutz women seem to be seeking to reassert their feminine status.

A woman's primary role is that of motherhood and most women have some or other of the attributes which fit them for this role. Consequently, the pursuit of a career for the mother of a young family is an arduous and conflict-ridden undertaking. Of course, there are ameliorative procedures that can be introduced – for example, extended maternity leave, state-run playgroups for all under-fives etc. – but these would only dent the tip of the iceberg. The physical, intellectual and emotional demands made upon the mother continue throughout the offsprings' childhood, unless one delegates entirely the role of mother to a substitute.

The conclusions of Gerson with respect to the kibbutz are remarkably similar to those of a Political and Economic Planning report on *Women in Top Jobs* (Fogarty *et al.*, 1971). This is a truly informative report and should be closely studied by all those interested in social reform or feminine psychology. Although the career women who were the subjects of this survey were highly motivated and involved in their work, they still felt that if a conflict between work and family should arise, the family would have priority. As one woman said: 'I have always said and meant that if some reason for leaving arose connected with my children (physical or psychological problems) they would come first.' In evaluating the relative performances of men and women, the report has this to say:

As regards highly qualified women generally, these studies support the finding from studies in other fields that the abilities and interests of men and women overlap considerably. They are not two separate worlds. They also indicate that the interests and abilities of women in the professions and management tend to differ from those of men in certain respects; so long as it is remembered that the differences are comparative, and that the point is not that all men and women have, or lack, certain characteristics but that the chances are rather greater that men will have some characteristics and women others. Women are more likely than men to have what might be called a general rather than a specialized (or a 'horizontal' rather than a 'vertical') type of ambition; to be interested in balancing family or leisure interests against work, and to settle for a satisfying job which leaves room for this rather than to drive towards the peaks of a profession. They tend to be less interested in empire-building, office politics, and administration. They are less likely than men to be forceful and competitive whether in their jobs or in promoting their own careers. They are seen as more likely to adopt an informal, personal, expressive style of management or professional approach, and as more tense, self-conscious, meticulous in details, and reluctant to delegate than men.

Moreover, it was not simply force of circumstance which determined that a fair proportion of women BBC producers worked in children's and educational programmes, only a tiny proportion in Current Affairs and none in Outside Broadcasts.

These several results suggest therefore that, despite equality of opportunity, men and women may forge rather different roles for themselves, socially and psychologically. This should occasion not surprise, but relief. It would be quite extraordinary indeed if male and female cognitive styles and orientations were totally at variance with their biological propensities. It is for these reasons that one views with some disquiet another of the oft-repeated demands of some feminist activists – that for twenty-four-hour crêches or nurseries to enable women with young children to continue in their employment. Apart from the adverse effects that may result from such institutions, there is a logical inconsistency inherent in such a demand. It lies in the fact that the staff of such nurseries, inevitably female, would be 'condemned' to relentless domesticity and care-taking, the very occupations of which the feminine liberators are unreservedly contemptuous. On the contrary, women with families are only able to pursue their careers with the aid of just such women.

In a most cogent article, Carlson (1972) says:

One need not accept, much less defend, the *status quo* in order to question whether it might not be an ultimate defeat for women to define themselves and their goals in terms of a masculine-hierarchical-competitive construction of experience. Yet this is implicit in current diagnoses of the problem as one of 'subjugation', and in the recommended remedies which would reject intrinsically femine qualities in demanding re-differentiation of sex roles in work, love and family experience.

It would be a pity indeed if women sought to make this less a man's world by repudiating their feminity and by striving for masculine goals. It seems that few women can or wish to compete in the competitive, assertive spheres of the male. As the final PEP report on the problems and prospects of career women points out:

To reach the top, as apart from reaching an interesting and responsible post at middle level, would as the women see it call for a 'maximum' commitment of time and energy, and so a sacrifice of other interests which they are not prepared to make (Fogarty, Rapoport and Rapoport, 1972).

But when they do compete, it is to be hoped that it is their ability, their skill and their contributions, rather than their sex, that are the salient considerations.

It is perhaps time women sought to redefine their roles, placing value and emphasis on their particular talents and skills. This would lead to different patterns of employment for men and women where necessary – the woman being able to leave her job temporarily, and without penalty, to have and raise her family. Too often otherwise the wife becomes the two-job partner; then, as an East German report complained, 'there is no time for free-time', and the human and emotional aspects of family life are invariably sacrificed. It is not surprising that employment itself is no longer considered the significant factor. As the 1972 P E P report observes:

A number of East European sources add the comment that the value of women's contribution to work lies not merely in more of the same sort of abilities and interests already supplied by men but in qualities complementary to those of men.

Nurturance, whether in the wider educational sense or in the narrower domestic sense, is and will remain women's forte. It is fortunate that many find contentment and fulfilment in just such a role, and it is important that they should not be deprecated for doing so, since on them depends the emotional security of future generations. For social reform, no better prescriptive guidelines can be found than the considered conclusions of the final P E P report:

The research team found no reason to suppose that dual careers or any other single pattern will or should become *the* convention for the future. The evidence on the contrary is that a range of patterns will be needed – among them the old traditional pattern of the housewife at home – to match the circumstances and personalities of different married couples. All will need to be equally legitimate and socially accepted. The problem will be not to impose one or other as a new stereotype but to facilitate the right choice among them all, and to help and equip married couples to manage their chosen pattern with a minimum of strain. This point of view, expressed in the reports, meets with no resistance from reviewers and to many appears to be strongly and positively acceptable.

References

ALLPORT, G. W., VERNON, P. E., and LINDZEY, G. (1951), *Study of Values*, Houghton Mifflin.

ANDREW, R. J., and ROGERS, L. (1972), 'Testosterone, search behaviour and persistence', *Nature*, in press.

ARCHER, J. (1971), 'Sex differences in emotional behaviour: a reply to Gray and Buffery', *Acta Psychologica*, vol. 35, pp. 415–29.

BANDURA, A., ROSS, D., and ROSS, S. (1961), 'Transmission of aggression through imitation of aggressive models', *J. abnorm. soc. Psychol.*, vol. 63, pp. 575–82.

BARR, M. L., and BERTRAM, E. G. (1949), 'A morphological distinction between neurones of the male and female, and the behaviour of the nucleolar satellite during accelerated nucleoprotein synthesis', *Nature*, vol. 163, pp. 676–7.

BEACH, F. A. (1942), 'Male and female mating behaviour in prepuberally castrated female rats treated with androgen', *Endocrinology*, vol. 31, pp. 673–8.

BEEMAN, E. A. (1947), 'The effect of male hormones on aggressive behaviour in mice', *Physiol. Zool.*, vol. 20, pp. 373–404.

BENNETT, G. K., SEASHORE, H. G., and WESMAN, A. G. (1959), *Differential Aptitude Tests*, Psychological Corporation, 3rd edn.

BERNARD, J. (1964), *Academic Women*, Pennsylvania State University Press.

BETTELHEIM, B. (1969), *The Children of the Dream*, Thames & Hudson.

BHAVNANI, R., and HUTT, C. (1972), 'Divergent thinking in boys and girls', *J. child psychol. Psychiat.*, in press.

BIERMAN, E. L. (1969), 'Oral contraceptives, lipoproteins and lipid transport', in H. A. Salhanick, D. M. Kipins and R.L. Vande Wiele (eds.), *Metabolic Effects of Gonadal Hormones and Contraceptive Steroids*, Plenum Press.

BRINDLEY, C., CLARKE, P., HUTT, C., ROBINSON, I., and WETHLI, E. (1972), 'Sex differences in the activities and social interactions of nursery school children' in R. P. Michael and J. H. Crook (eds.), *Comparative Ecology and Behaviour of Primates*, Academic Press, in press.

BRONSON, F. H., and DESJARDINS, C. (1971), 'Steroid hormones and aggressive behaviour in mammals' in B. E. Eleftheriou and J. P. Scott (eds.), *The Physiology of Aggression and Defeat*, Plenum Press.

BROVERMAN, D. M., KLAIBER, E. L., KOBAYASHI, Y., and VOGEL, W. (1968), 'Roles of activation and inhibition in sex differences in cognitive abilities', *Psychol. Rev.*, vol. 75, pp. 23–50.

BROWN, J. H. U., and BARKER, S. B. (1966), *Basic Endocrinology*, F. A. Davis Co., 2nd edn.

BUFFERY, A. W. H., and GRAY, J. A. (1972), 'Sex differences in the development of perceptual and linguistic skills', in C. Ounsted and D. C. Taylor (eds.), *Gender Differences: Their Ontogeny and Significance*, Churchill.

CAMERON, J., LIVSON, N., and BAYLEY, N. (1967), 'Infant vocalisations and their relationship to mature intelligence', *Science*, vol. 157, pp. 331–3.

CARLSON, E. R., and CARLSON, R. (1960), 'Male and female subjects in personality research', *J. abnorm. soc. Psychol.*, vol. 61, pp. 482–3.

CARLSON, R. (1965), 'Stability and change in the adolescent's self-image', *Child Devel.*, vol. 36, pp. 659–66.

CARLSON, R. (1971), 'Sex differences in ego functioning: exploratory studies of agency and communion', *J. consult. clin. Psychol.*, vol. 37, pp. 267–77.

CARLSON, R. (1972), 'Understanding women: implications for personality theory and research', *J. soc. Issues*, in press.

CLARK, A. H., WYON, S. M., and RICHARDS, M. P. M. (1969), 'Free-play in nursery school children', *J. child Psychol. Psychiat.*, vol. 10, pp. 205–16.

COLLEY, T. (1959), 'The nature and origin of psychological sexual identity', *Psychol. Rev.*, vol. 66, pp. 165–77.

COLLIAS, N. E. (1944), 'Aggressive behaviour among vertebrate animals', *Physiol. Zool.*, vol. 17, pp. 83–123.

CONEL, J. L. (1963), *The Postnatal Development of the Human Cerebral Cortex*, Harvard University Press.

CONNER, R. L., and LEVINE, S. (1969), 'Hormonal influences on aggressive behaviour', in S. Garattini and E. B. Sigg (eds.), *Aggressive Behaviour*, Excerpta Medica Foundation.

CONNER, R. L., LEVINE, S., WERTHEIM, G. A., and CUMMER, J. F. (1969), 'Hormonal determinants of aggressive behaviour', *Ann. N. Y. Acad. Sci.*, vol. 159, pp. 760–76.

DALE, R. R. (1970), 'A comparison of the academic performance of male and female students in schools and universities', *J. biosoc. Science Suppl.*, vol. 2, pp. 95–9.

DALTON, K. (1968), 'Ante-natal progesterone and intelligence' *Brit. J. Psychiat.*, vol. 114, pp. 1377–81.

DALTON, K. (1969), *The Menstrual Cycle*, Penguin.

DAVIES, B. T. (1970), 'Comparative employability of men and women in different industries', *J. biosoc. Science Suppl.*, vol. 2, pp. 101–6.

DAWSON, J. L. M. (1967a), 'Cultural and physiological influence upon spatial-perceptual processes in West Africa: Part I', *Int. J. Psychol.*, vol. 2, pp. 115–28.

DAWSON, J. L. M. (1967b), 'Cultural and physiological influences upon spatial-perceptual processes in West Africa, Part II', *Int. J. Psychol.*, vol. 2, pp. 171–85.

DONOVAN, B. T. (1970), *Mammalian Neuroendocrinology*, McGraw-Hill.

DOUGLAS, J. W. B., ROSS, J. M., and SIMPSON, H. R. (1968), *All Our Future*, Peter Davies.

DOUVAN, E. (1960), 'Sex differences in adolescent character processes', *Merrill-Palmer Q.*, vol. 6, pp. 203–11.

ECKERT, H. M. (1970), 'Visual-motor tasks at 3 and 4 years of age', *Percept. Mot. Skills*, vol. 31, p. 560.

EHRHARDT, A. A., EPSTEIN, R., and MONEY, J. (1968), 'Fetal androgens and female gender identity in the early-treated adrenogenital syndrome', *Johns Hopkins med. J.*, vol. 122, pp. 160–67.

FEDERMAN, M. D. (1967), *Abnormal Sexual Development*, Saunders.

FESHBACH, S. (1970), 'Aggression', in P. Mussen (ed.), *Carmichael's Manual of Child Psychology*, vol. 2, Wiley.

FOGARTY, M., ALLEN, A. J., ALLEN, I., and WALTERS, P. (1971), *Women in Top Jobs*, Allen & Unwin.

FOGARTY, M., RAPOPORT, R., and RAPOPORT, R. (1972), *Women and Top Jobs: The Next Move*, PEP Broadsheet, no. 535.

FREEDMAN, D. G. (1971), 'Genetic variations on the hominid theme: individual, sex and ethnic differences', paper to the First Symposium of the International Society for the Study of Behavioural Development, Nijmegen, July.

FRYE, B. E. (1967), *Hormonal Control in Vertebrates*, Macmillan Co.

GALTON, F. (1894), 'The relative sensitivity of men and women at the nape of the neck by Webster's test', *Nature*, vol. 50, pp. 40–42.

GARAI, J. E., and SCHEINFELD, A. (1968), 'Sex differences in mental and behavioural traits', *Genet. psychol. Monogr.*, vol. 77, pp. 169–299.

GERALL, A. A. (1963), 'The effect of prenatal and postnatal injections of testosterone proprionate on prepuberal male guinea pig sexual behaviour', *J. comp. physiol. Psychol.*, vol. 56, pp. 92–5.

GERSON, M. (1971), 'Women in the kibbutz', *Amer. J. Orthopsychiat.*, vol. 41, pp. 566–73.

GOY, R. W. (1968), 'Organising effects of androgen on the behaviour of rhesus monkeys', in R. P. Michael (ed.), *Endocrinology and Human Behaviour*, Oxford University Press.

GOY, R. W., MITCHELL, J. C., and YOUNG, W. C. (1962), 'Effect of testosterone proprionate on O_2 consumption of female and female pseudohermaphroditic guinea pigs', *Amer. Zool.*, vol. 2, p. 525.

GRAM, T. E., and GILLETTE, J. R. (1969), 'The role of sex hormones in the metabolism of drugs and other foreign compounds by hepatic microsomal enzymes', in H. A. Salhanick, D. M. Kipnis and R. L. Vande Wiele (eds.), *Metabolic Effects of Gonadal Hormones and Contraceptive Steroids*, Plenum Press.

GREENE, R. (1970), *Human Hormones*, Weidenfeld & Nicolson.

GUILFORD, J. P. (1967), *The Nature of Human Intelligence*, McGraw-Hill.

GUTMANN, D. (1965), 'Women and the conception of ego strength', *Merrill-Palmer Q.*, vol. 11, pp. 229–40.

HAMBURG, D. A. (1971), 'Psychobiological studies of aggressive behaviour', *Nature*, vol. 230, pp. 19–23.

HAMPSON, J. L. (1965), 'Determinants of psychosexual orientation', in F. A. Beach (ed.), *Sex and Behaviour*, Wiley.

HARLOW, H. (1965), 'Sexual behaviour of the rhesus monkey', in F. A. Beach (ed.), *Sex and Behaviour*, Wiley.

HARRIS, G. W. (1964), 'Sex hormones, brain development and brain function', *Endocrinology*, vol. 75, pp. 627–48.

HARRIS, G. W. (1970), 'Hormonal differentiation of the developing central nervous system with respect to patterns of endocrine function', *Phil. Trans. roy. Soc. Lond.*, vol. 259, pp. 165–77.

HARRIS, G. W., and JACOBSOHN, D. (1952), 'Functional grafts of the anterior pituitary gland', *Proc. roy. Soc.*, vol. 139, pp. 263–76.

HARRIS, G. W., and LEVINE, S. (1965), 'Sexual differentiation of the brain and its experimental control', *J. Physiol.*, vol. 181, pp. 379–400.

HEIM, A. H. (1970), *Intelligence and Personality*, Penguin.

HOVLAND, C. I., and JANIS, I. L. (eds.), (1959), *Personality and Persuasibility*, Yale University Press.

HUNT, E. E. (1966), 'The developmental genetics of man', in F. Falkner (ed.), *Human Development*, Saunders.

HUTT, C. (1970a), 'Specific and diversive exploration', in H. Reese and L. Lipsitt (eds.), *Advances in Child Development and Behaviour*, vol. V, Academic Press.

HUTT, C. (1970b), 'Curiosity in young children', *Science J.*, vol. 6, pp. 68–72.

HUTT, C. (1972a), 'Neuroendocrinological, behavioural and intellectual aspects of sexual differentiation in human development', in C. Ounsted and D. C. Taylor (eds.), *Gender Differences: Their Ontogeny and Significance*, Churchill, in press.

HUTT, C. (1972b), 'Sex differences in human development', *Hum. Devel.*, vol. 15, pp. 153–70.

HUTT, C. (1972c), 'Sexual dimorphism: its significance in human development', in F. Mönks, W. Hartup and J. de Wit (eds.), *Determinants of Behavioural Development*, Academic Press.

HUTT, C., and BHAVNANI, R. (1972), 'Predictions from play', *Nature*, in press.

HUTT, C., and VAIZEY, M. J. (1966), 'Differential effects of group density on social behaviour', *Nature*, vol. 209, pp. 1371–2.

HUTT, S. J., and HUTT, C. (1970), *Direct Observation and Measurement of Behaviour*, C. C. Thomas.

JOLLY, C. J. (1970), 'The seed-eaters: a new model of hominid differentiation based on a baboon analogy', *Man*, vol. 5, pp. 5–26.

JONES, H. E. (1949), *Motor Performance and Growth: A Developmental Study of Static Dynamometric Strength*, University of California Press.

JOST, A. (1953), 'Problems of fetal endocrinology: the gonadal and hypophyseal hormones', *Recent Progress in Hormone Res.*, vol. 8, pp. 379–418.

JOST, A. (1960), 'Hormonal influences in the sex development of bird and mammalian embryos', in *Sex Differentiation and Development*, Mem. Soc. Endocrinol., no. 7, Cambridge University Press.

KAGAN, J. (1969), 'On the meaning of behaviour: illustrations from the infant', *Child Devel.*, vol. 40, pp. 1121–34.

KAPLAN, A. R. (1967), 'Sex-chromatin variations in institutionalised females: prisoners, confined juvenile offenders and non-institutionalised volunteers', in J. Wortis (ed.), *Recent Advances in Biological Psychiatry*, vol. 9, Plenum Press.

KAPPAS, A., and SONG, C. S. (1969), 'Sex hormones, the gastrointestinal tract and the liver', in H. A. Salhanick, D. M. Kipnis and R. L. Vande Wiele (eds.), *Metabolic Effects of Gonadal Hormones and Contraceptive Steroids*, Plenum Press.

KIMURA, D. (1961), 'Cerebral dominance and the perception of verbal stimuli', *Canad. J. Psychol.*, vol. 15, pp. 166–71.

KIMURA, D. (1963), 'Speech lateralisation in young children as determined by an auditory test', *J. compar. physiol. Psychol.*, vol. 56, pp. 899–902.

KIMURA, D. (1964), 'Left-right differences in the perception of melodies', *Q. J. exper. Psychol.*, vol. 16, pp. 355–8.

KLAIBER, E. L., BROVERMAN, D. M., VOGEL, W., ABRAHAM, G. E., and CONE, F. L. (1971), 'Effects of infused testosterone on mental performances and serum LH', *J. clin. endocrin. Metab.*, vol. 32, pp. 341–9.

KNOX, C., and KIMURA, D. (1970), 'Cerebral processing of nonverbal sounds in boys and girls', *Neuropsychologia*, vol. 8, pp. 227–37.

KORNER, A. F. (1969), 'Neonatal startles, smiles, erections and reflex sucks as related to state, sex and individuality', *Child Devel.*, vol. 40, pp. 1039–53.

LADOSKY, W., and GAZIRI, L. C. J. (1969), 'Brain serotonin and sexual differentiation of the nervous system', *Neuroendocrinology*, vol. 6, pp. 168–74.

LEJEUNE, J. (1967), 'Chromosomal studies in psychiatry', in J. Wortis (ed.), *Recent Advances in Biological Psychiatry*, vol. 9, Plenum Press.

LEVINE, S. (1966), 'Sex differences in the brain', *Scientific Amer.*, vol. 214, pp. 84–90.

LIPSITT, L. P., and LEVY, N. (1959), 'Electrotactual threshold in the neonate', *Child Devel.*, vol. 30, pp. 547–54.

LISK, R. D. (1962), 'Testosterone-sensitive centres in the hypothalamus of the rat', *Acta Endocrinol.*, vol. 41, pp. 195–204.

LITTLE, B. (1968), 'Psychospecialisation: functions of differential interest in persons and things', *Bull. Brit. psychol. Soc.*, vol. 21, p. 113A.

LYON, M. F. (1962), 'Sex chromatin and gene action in the mammalian X-chromosome', *Amer. J. hum. Genet.*, vol. 14, p. 135.

MACCOBY, E. E. (ed.) (1966), *The Development of Sex Differences*, Tavistock.

MASTERS, W. H., and JOHNSON, V. E. (1965), 'The sexual response cycles of the human male and female: comparative anatomy and physiology', in F. A. Beach (ed.), *Sex and Behaviour*, Wiley.

McGREW, W. C. (1972), 'Aspects of social development in nursery school children with emphasis on introduction to the group', in N. Blurton-Jones (ed.), *Ethological Studies of Child Behaviour*, Cambridge University Press, in press.

MENDEL, G. (1965), 'Children's preferences for differing degrees of novelty', *Child Devel.*, vol. 36, pp. 453–65.

MICHAEL, R. P. (1962), 'Oestrogen-sensitive neurones and sexual behaviour in female cats', *Science*, vol. 136, pp. 322–3.

MISCHEL, W. (1970), 'Sex-typing and socialisation', in P. Mussen (ed.), *Carmichael's Manual of Child Psychology*, vol. 2, Wiley.

MITTWOCH, U. (1971), 'Sex determination in birds and mammals', *Nature*, vol. 231, pp. 432–4.

MONEY, J. (1963), 'Cytogenetic and psychosexual incongruities with a note on space-form blindness', *Amer. J. Psychiat.*, vol. 119, pp. 820–27.

MONEY, J. (1965), 'Influence of hormones on sexual behaviour', *Annual Rev. Med.*, vol. 16, pp. 67–82.

MONEY, J. (1970), 'Sexual dimorphism and homosexual gender identity', *Psychol. Bull*, vol. 74, pp. 425–40.

MONEY, J. (1971), 'Psychologic findings associated with the XO, XXY and XYY anomalies', *Southern med. J.*, vol. 64, suppl. 1, pp. 59–64.

MONEY, J., and EHRHARDT, A. A. (1968), 'Prenatal hormonal exposure: possible effects on behaviour in man', in R. P. Michael (ed.), *Endocrinology and Human Behaviour*, Oxford University Press.

MONEY, J., HAMPSON, J. G., and HAMPSON, J. L. (1955), 'Hermaphroditism: recommendations concerning assignment of sex, change of sex, and psychologic management', *Bull. Johns Hopkins Hospital*, vol. pp.97, 284–300.

MONEY, J., HAMPSON, J. G., and HAMPSON, J. L. (1957), 'Imprinting and the establishment of gender role', *Arch. Neurol. Psychiat.*, vol. 77, pp. 333–6.

MOORE, T. (1967), 'Language and intelligence: a longitudinal study of the first eight years. Part I: patterns of development in boys and girls', *Hum. Devel.*, vol. 10, pp. 88–106.

MOSS, H. (1967), 'Sex, age and state as determinants of mother–infant interaction', *Merrill-Palmer Q.*, vol. 13, pp. 19–36.

NEGULICI, E., CHRISTODIRESCU, D., and ALEXANDRU, S. (1968), 'Psychological aspects of the testicular feminisation syndrome', *Psychosom. Med.*, vol. 30, pp. 45–50.

NEUMANN, F., and ELGER, W. (1966), 'Permanent changes in gonadal function and sexual behaviour as a result of early feminisation of male rats by treatment with an antiandrogenic steroid', *Endokrinologie*, vol. 50, pp. 209–25.

NEUMANN, F., STEINBECK, H., and HAHN, J. D. (1970), 'Hormones and brain differentiation', in L. Martini, M. Motta and F. Fraschini (eds.), *The Hypothalamus*, Academic Press.

NICOLSON, A. B., and HANLEY, C. (1953), 'Indices of physiological maturity: derivation and interrelationships', *Child Devel.*, vol. 24, pp. 3–38.

NOTERMANS, S. L. H., and TOPHOPF, M. M. W. A. (1967), 'Sex difference in pain tolerance and pain apperception', *Psychiatria, Neurologia, Neurochirurgia*, vol. 70, pp. 23–9.

OETZEL, R. M. (1966), 'Classified summary of research in sex differences', in E. E. Maccoby (ed.), *The Development of Sex Differences*, Tavistock.

OUNSTED, C., and TAYLOR, D. C. (1972), 'The Y-chromosome message: a point of view', in C. Ounsted and D. C. Taylor (eds.) *Gender Differences: Their Ontogeny and Significance*, Churchill.

PERSKY, H., SMITH, K. D., and BASU, G. K. (1971), 'Relation of psychologic measures of aggression and hostility to testostere production in man', *Psychosom. Med.*, vol. 33, pp. 265–77.   uo

PHOENIX, C. H., GOY, R. W., GERALL, A. A., and YOUNG, W. C. (1959), 'Organising action of prenatally administered testosterone proprionate on the tissues mediating mating behaviour in the female guinea pig', *Endocrinology*, vol. 65, pp. 369–82.

PHOENIX, C. H., GOY, R. W., and RESKO, J. A. (1968), 'Psychosexual differentiation as a function of androgenic stimulation', in M. Diamond (ed.), *Perspectives in Reproduction and Sexual Behaviour*, Indiana University Press.

POLANI, P. (1970), 'Chromosome phenotypes – sex chromosomes', in F. C. Fraser and V. A. McKuisick (eds.), *Congenital Malformations*, Excerpta Medica.

POTTS, D. M. (1970), 'Which is the weaker sex?', *J. biosoc. Science*, suppl. 2, pp. 147–57.

RAISMAN, G., and FIELD, P. M. (1971), 'Sexual dimorphism in the preoptic area of the rat', *Science*, vol. 173, pp. 731–3.

ROSE, R. H., HOLADAY, J. W. and BERNSTEIN, I. S. (1971), 'Plasma testosterone dominance rank and aggressive behaviour in male rhesus monkeys', *Nature*, vol. 231, pp. 366–8.

ROSSI, A. S. (1965), 'Women in science: why so few?', *Science*, vol. 148, pp. 1196–9.

SCHAEFER, L. E. (1964), 'Serum cholesterol – triglyceride distribution in a "normal" New York City population', *Amer. J. Med.*, vol. 36, pp. 262–8.

SCHALLER, G. B. (1965), 'Behavioural comparisons of the apes', in I. de Vore (ed.), *Primate Behaviour*, Holt, Rinehart & Winston.

SCHEINFELD, A. (1965), *Your Heredity and Environment*, Lippincott.

SHIMADA, H., and GORBMAN, A. (1970), 'Long lasting changes in RNA synthesis in the forebrains of female rats treated with testosterone soon after birth', *Biochem. Biophys. Res. Comm.*, vol. 38, pp. 423–30.

SHORTELL, J. R., and BILLER, H. B. (1970), 'Aggression in children as a function of sex of subject and sex of opponent', *Devel. Psychol.*, vol. 3, pp. 143–4.

SHOUKSMITH, G. (1970), *Intelligence, Creativity and Cognitive Style*, Batsford.

SIMNER, M. L. (1971), 'Newborn's response to the cry of another infant', *Devel. Psychol.*, vol. 5, pp. 136–50.

SMOCK, C. D., and HOLT, B. G. (1962), 'Children's reactions to novelty: an experimental study of "curiosity motivation"', *Child Devel.*, vol. 33, pp. 631–42.

STAFFORD, R. E. (1961), 'Sex differences in spatial visualisation as evidence of sex linked inheritance', *Percept. Mot. Skills*, vol. 13, p. 428.

SUCHOWSKY, G. K., PEGRASSI, L., and BONSIGNORI, A. (1969), 'The effect of steroids on aggressive behaviour in isolated male mice', in S. Garattini and E. B. Sigg (eds.), *Aggressive Behaviour*, Excerpta Medica Foundation.

SUOMI, S. J., SACKETT, G. P., and HARLOW, H. S. (1970), 'Development of sex preference in rhesus monkeys', *Devel. Psychol.*, vol. 3, pp. 326–36.

TANNER, J. M. (1970), 'Physical growth', in P. H. Mussen (ed.), *Carmichael's Manual of Child Psychology*, vol. 1, Wiley.

TANNER, J. M., WHITEHOUSE, R. H., and TAKAISHI, M. (1966), 'Standards from birth to maturity for height, weight, height velocity and weight velocity: British children 1965', *Arch. Dis. Childhood*, vol. 41, pp. 454–71, 613–35.

TAYLOR, D. C. (1969), 'Differential rates of cerebral maturation between sexes and between hemispheres', *Lancet*, 19 July, pp. 140–2.

TAYLOR, S. P., and EPSTEIN, S. (1967), 'Aggression as a function of the interaction of the sex of the aggressor and sex of the victim', *J. Person.*, vol. 35, pp. 474–86.

TERMAN, L. M. (1947), 'Psychological approaches to the biography of genius', *Papers on Eugenics*, no. 4, pp. 3–20. Reprinted in P. E. Vernon (ed.), *Creativity*, Penguin.

TERMAN, L. M., and TYLER, L. E. (1954), 'Psychological sex differences', in L. Carmichael (ed.), *Manual of Child Psychology*, Wiley, 2nd edn.

TOLLMAN, J., and KING, J. A. (1956), 'The effects of testosterone proprionate on aggression in male and female C27BL/10 mice', *Brit. J. Anim. Behav.*, vol. 4, pp. 147–9.

TYLER, L. (1965), *The Psychology of Human Differences*, Appleton-Century-Crofts, 3rd edn.

VOGEL, W., BROVERMAN, D. M., KLAIBER, E. L., ABRAHAM, G., and CONE, F. L. (1971), 'Effects of testosterone infusions upon EEGs of normal male adults', *Electroenceph. clin. Neurophysiol.*, vol. 31, pp. 400–403.

WALBERG, H. J. (1969), 'Physics, feminity and creativity', *Devel. Psychol.*, vol. 1, pp. 47–54.

WALLACH, M. A., and KOGAN, N. (1965), *Modes of Thinking in Young Children*, Holt, Rinehart & Winston.

WATSON, J. S. (1969), 'Operant conditioning of visual fixation in infants under visual and auditory reinforcement', *Devel. Psychol.*, vol. 1, pp. 508–16.

WECHSLER, D. (1941), *The Measurement of Adult Intelligence*, Williams & Wilkins.

WECHSLER, D. (1958), *The Measurement and Appraisal of Adult Intelligence*, Williams & Wilkins, 4th edn.

WELCH, B. L. (1967), Discussion following A. B. Rothballer, 'Aggression, defense and neurohumors', in C. D. Clemente and D. B. Lindsley (eds.), *Aggression and Defense – Neural Mechanisms and Social Patterns*, University of California Press.

WHALEN, R. E. (1968), 'Differentiation of the neural mechanisms which control gonadotropin secretion and sexual behaviour', in M. Diamond (ed.), *Perspectives in Reproduction and Sexual Behaviour*, Indiana University Press.

WHITING, B. (ed.) (1963), *Six Cultures: Studies of Child Rearing*, Wiley.

WHITING, J. W. M. (1965), Discussion following J. L. Hampson, 'Determinants of psychosexual orientation', in F. A. Beach (ed.), *Sex and Behaviour*, Wiley.

WITKIN, H. A., DYK, R. B., FATERSON, H. F., GOODENOUGH, D. R., and KARP, S. A. (1962), *Psychological Differentiation*, Wiley.

WYNNE-EDWARDS, V. C. (1962), *Animal Dispersion in Relation to Social Behaviour*, Oliver & Boyd.

YOUNG, H. B. (1963), 'Ageing and adolescence', *Devel. Med. Child Neurol.*, vol. 5, pp. 451–60.

YOUNG, W. C. (1965), 'The organisation of sexual behaviour by hormonal action during the prenatal and larval periods in vertebrates', in F. A. Beach (ed.), *Sex and Behaviour*, Wiley.

Acknowledgements

Acknowledgement is due to the following for permission to use figures in this volume.

Figures 1, 3, and 4 George Weidenfeld & Nicholson. Figure 2 The Macmillan Co. New York. Figure 5 *American Journal of Medicine* and L E Schaefer. Figures 7, 9, 10, 11, 12, 13, 14 and 15 John Wiley & Sons Inc. Figure 8 *Endocrinology*. Figures 16, 17, 18, 19 and 20 Oxford University Press. Figure 21 John Wiley & Sons Ltd. Figure 22 Spastics International Medical Publications. Figure 23 *Archives of Disease in Childhood* and J M Tanner. Figure 24 The Society for Research in Child Development Inc. and Dr C Hanley. Figure 26 and 33 Appleton-Century-Crofts. Figure 28 Pergamon Press Ltd. Figures 29 and 30 *Annals of New York Academy of Science*. Figure 31 *Psychosomatic Medicine*. Figures 32 and 34 Academic Press Inc.

Index